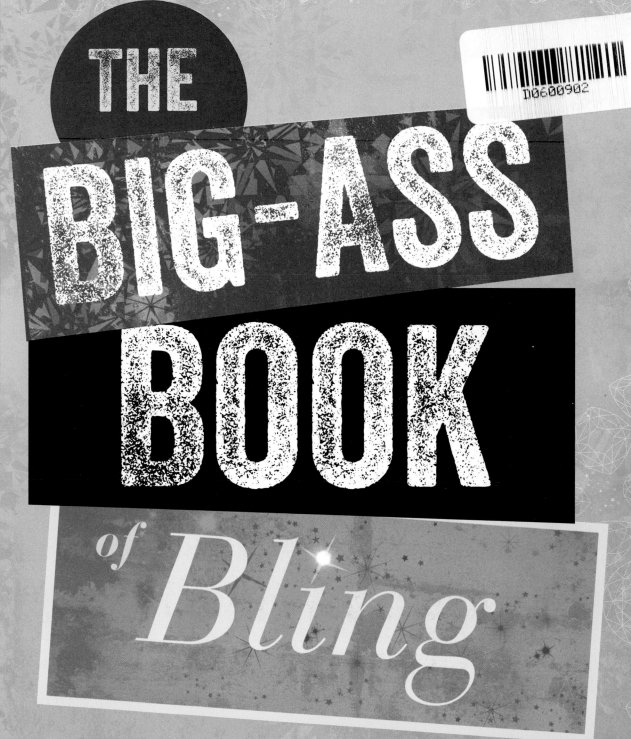

# THE BIG-ASS BOOK of Bling

*by* **MARK MONTANO**

**G**

**GALLERY BOOKS**

New York   London   Toronto   Sydney   New Delhi

**Also by Mark Montano**

*Pulp Fiction: Perfect Paper Projects*
*Vision Box Idea Book*
*The Big-Ass Book of Home Décor*
*The Big-Ass Book of Crafts*
*The Big-Ass Book of Crafts 2*
*CosmoGirl: Cool Room*
*Dollar Store Décor*
*Super Suite*
*Window Treatments & Slipcovers for Dummies*
*While You Were Out: The Rooms, the Cast, the Dreams*

G

**Gallery Books**
A Division of Simon & Schuster, Inc.
1230 Avenue of the Americas
New York, NY 10020

First Gallery Books trade paperback edition November 2012

GALLERY BOOKS and colophon are registered trademarks of Simon & Schuster, Inc.

For information about special discounts for bulk purchases,
please contact Simon & Schuster Special Sales at 1-866-506-1949
or business@simonandschuster.com.

The Simon & Schuster Speakers Bureau can bring authors to
your live event. For more information or to book an event contact
the Simon & Schuster Speakers Bureau at 1-866-248-3049 or
visit our website at www.simonspeakers.com.

Designed by Jane Archer/www.psbella.com

Manufactured in the United States of America

10  9  8  7  6  5  4  3  2  1

Library of Congress Cataloging-in-Publication Data

Montano, Mark.
The big-ass book of bling / Mark Montano.
p. cm.
1. Hip-hop jewelry. I. Title.
TT212.M658 2012
745.594'2—dc23
2012022974

ISBN 978-1-4516-8528-2
ISBN 978-1-4516-8529-9 (ebook)

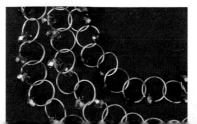

# ConTents

## NOTE TO READERS

This book is dedicated to my
parents, who indulged me
every birthday and holiday with as
many arts and craft supplies
as they could afford.

# HELLO
## EVERYONE!

I've just come back from a very long trip down memory lane while writing this book. I was able to relive twenty years of my life as a fashion designer in New York City. Before I showed my collections in the big tents in Bryant Park (now held in Lincoln Center), I owned a boutique for eighteen years and lived above it, in the heart of the East Village.

It was an amazing life. Every day (and I mean *every* day) I would get up, design and make dresses, make jewelry, and make a living doing the things I loved. When I went home at night, I would make more things with which to decorate my apartment. It was, and still is, the way I live my life—

### creativity from morning till night.

I think it's what keeps me sane!

Making jewelry and accessories for my boutique was often what kept me afloat financially. Even if I didn't sell a single dress some days, I would always sell a few pairs of earrings or a necklace. But they were more than moneymakers, they were just fun to create. I used whatever I had, too. Extra buttons, fabric and leather scraps, zippers—you name it, I made it into an accessory! Soon I realized that making my own accessories was what made my collections more exciting during Fashion Week, so they became part of my line. I also realized that, on the runway,

## *Bling is* BETTER!

### Sparkle and shine make for an exciting presentation!

Since accessories are a question of taste, I want you to look with your own creative eye at what I've made in this book. Look at the techniques and ingredients and see what you can do with the projects. You don't have to make them exactly the way I did. In fact, I'm positive you can turn them into pieces that will scream your name and express your own personal style. Take the creativity, inspiration, and techniques you find in this book and make your own jewelry line or reinvent your wardrobe. Look at this as a jumping-off point to how amazing you are!

This is the first book in which I've recommended products that I believe will change the way you think about creativity. For example, I feature a **microwave kiln** for fusing glass. I've been playing with mine for two years now and finally decided it was something that you should know about. It's brilliant and I absolutely love it. I've also experimented with **molds and mold-making**. For some reason, I was afraid of diving into this type of craft. But now that I've actually tried it, it's the easiest thing I've ever done. It's like playing with Silly Putty. Yes, that easy! I ripped apart my house, looking for things to make into molds and then proceeded to cast them by the hundreds. I couldn't stop! I think you'll feel the same way, too, once you realize how easy it is.

On a side note, I only recommend products that work and are the best of the best! So in this book is my list of tried-and-true products that will make your projects a success. The Resource Guide section gives you a list of terrific manufacturers who make a variety of top-of-the-line products, and the Things I Used section is a list of different materials I use in this book and that I use on a regular basis for crafting. Some of the items are made by specific manufacturers, but many of them can be purchased almost anywhere. As always, I encourage you to

# *have* FUN, *make* MESSES, *and* CREATE!

Know that perfection is overrated, and that your heart and soul are what will make your creations special. Remember, I'm always here for you at MARKMONTANONYC@AOL.COM.

**y** dad can sew better than I can, and though I don't like to toot my own horn, that's saying A LOT! He decided one day that, to make extra money for our family, he would start

doing upholstery along with his other business, which at the time was fixing cars. I owe a lot of my creativity and fearlessness—along with my ability to make really unfunny jokes—to my dad. For me, the best part of my dad's upholstery work was the scraps of vinyl I got to use in my crafty projects! Making vinyl flowers was my favorite, and the projects in this chapter remind me of much simpler times in my life.

# EVERLASTING FLOWER CUFF

Every time I see a flower on someone's wrist I think of old-fashioned wrist corsages. I recall seeing a box of corsages that someone had saved at a thrift store once, and each one had a handwritten tag on it with the occasion at which it was worn. I often think of a white-haired woman looking in that box and thinking back on her first date, her first dance, and the first time she fell in love. Hopefully this cuff will inspire similar memories someday!

## YOU'LL NEED

- 2½-inch flat metal cuff
- Lumiere metallic paint in a color that goes with your vinyl or leather (I used burgundy)
- ½-inch wide paintbrush
- ¼ yard altogether of vinyl or leather, in two different colors
- Scissors
- E-6000 glue
- Fiskars pinking shears
- 1 yard of leather, suede, or faux suede lace in a color that goes with your vinyl or leather
- Hot glue gun and glue sticks
- Large pin
- 14 inches of 20-gauge wire
- Needle-nose pliers (and wirecutters if the pliers don't have them)
- 7 pearl beads

## HERE'S HOW

**1** Paint your metal cuff with Lumiere metallic paint and let dry.

**2** Using regular scissors, cut your flowers out of the leather or vinyl, using the patterns on page 367. You will need five of them: two large, two medium, and one small.

**3** Glue them together with E-6000.

**4** Using pinking shears, cut seven small circles out of the vinyl, about 1 to 1½ inches in diameter.

**5** Roll your leather or suede lace into spiral disks (like a cinnamon bun) that fit inside the circles, then glue them down with the glue gun as shown in photo c.

**6** Poke a hole in the center of each circle with a large pin.

**7** Cut off a 2-inch piece of wire and make a tiny loop on the end. Place a pearl on it and poke it through the top center of one of the spiral disks. Do this for each disk.

**8** On six of the spiral disks, bend the wire so it's flat on the back of the disk.

**9** Poke a hole through the flower with the safety pin and then push the remaining, unbent pearl through, until the disk is nicely flush. Bend the wire in the back to keep it in place on the flower.

**10** Glue the bottom layer of your flower to the cuff first using E-6000 and then dab hot glue around the edges to hold it in place while the E-6000 dries.

**11** Glue three disks on each side of the cuff with E-6000 and let dry.

# EVERLASTING FLOWER HEADBAND

I've often wondered why girls are the only ones who get to wear flowers in their hair. I mean, I love flowers and sometimes I wish I could wear them in *my* hair—in public, anyway! I'm pretty sure there were some long-haired hippies back in the '60s pulling off a flower child look. How did we get so conservative?

## YoU'LL NEeD

- Plastic headband
- Hot glue gun and glue sticks
- 1 roll of cord in a color that goes with your vinyl or leather
- ⅛ yard each of vinyl or leather, in two different colors
- Scissors
- Fiskars pinking shears
- E-6000 glue
- 5 inches of 20-gauge wire
- Needle-nose pliers (and wirecutters if the pliers don't have them)
- 1 crystal bead
- Large pin
- 1 yard of leather, suede, or faux suede lace in a color that matches your vinyl or leather

## HeRE's HoW

**1** Dab a tiny bit of hot glue on the inside tip of your headband (starting at either end) and begin wrapping cord around the band, adding dots of hot glue on the inside as you continue wrapping as shown in photo a.

**2** Using regular scissors, cut your flowers using the patterns on page 367. You will need six of them: two large, three medium, and one small.

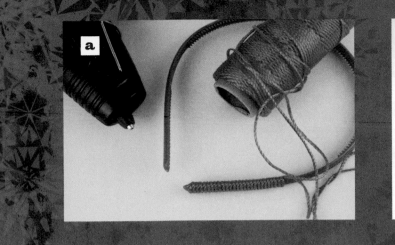

3. Using pinking shears, cut two two small circles—one from each of your colors of vinyl or leather—about 1 and 1½ inches in diameter, respectively.

4. Stack all of the pieces except for one medium flower, from the largest to the smallest, with the circles on top. Glue all the pieces together with E-6000.

5. Cut off a 5-inch piece of wire, bend a small loop at the very end, and string on your crystal bead.

6. Poke a hole through the center of all of the layers of your flower with a safety pin, and then push the wire with the crystal bead through it. Bend the wire in the back to keep everything in place and to secure all of the flower pieces together.

7. Cut a piece of vinyl about 5 inches long and 2½ inches wide. Fringe it with scissors.

8. Cut several 5-inch-long strips out of your leather or suede lace.

9. Sandwich the strips of lace in between the fringed piece and the flower, and glue together with E-6000 and hot glue. Dab the E-6000 on your pieces and then use dabs of hot glue to keep it in place while the E-6000 is drying.

10. Glue the remaining flower to the back of the ornament to make it nice and neat.

11. Glue the entire piece to the headband and let dry.

# ARCHERY SHOE CLIPS

I love everything about archery: the huge targets, the bows, and especially the arrows, with the beautiful feathered tips. I love that at the turn of the century, women would compete in this sport wearing beautiful dresses and corsets. These shoe clips remind me of that era.

## YOU'LL NEED

- Vinyl or leather in two different colors
- Scissors
- Circle stencils or several glasses of different sizes
- Fiskars pinking shears
- E-6000 glue
- Feathers that match your vinyl (I used feather duster feathers for the small clips and rooster feathers for the larger clips. www.createforless.com is a great source for feathers!)
- 2 clip-on earring blanks
- 2 flat-back acrylic gems for the centers of the clips

## HERE'S HOW
## FOR THE LARGE BLACK AND SILVER CLIPS

**1** Cut a square about 6 inches by 6 inches from both colors of your vinyl or leather. Trace four circles in various sizes on the back of the vinyl, keeping your alternating color palette in mind.

**2** Cut out the circles with pinking shears.

**3** Glue the three largest circles together using E-6000 and let dry.

**4** Glue feathers on the back of the smallest circle.

**5** Glue that on top of the three large circles.

**6** Top off with a gem and let dry.

**7** Turn the circles over and glue the clip-on earring blank to the back on the upper end of the circle. IMPORTANT! Do not put glue on the flat disk part of the earring! Glue on the scalloped part. The flat part has to rest comfortably against your foot.

**8** Repeat steps 1 through 7 for your second clip.

## HERE'S HOW
## FOR THE SMALLER CLIPS

**1** Cut two small circles in your vinyl and glue them together using E-6000.

**2** Glue the feather and clip-on earring blank on the upper part of the circle and let dry.

**3** Repeat steps 1 and 2 to make your second clip.

# BLOOMING FUSION

Scraps of leather, vinyl, and chain make up this large-and-in-charge piece. Add more flowers, change the colors, use silver chain instead . . . shake it up! Make one that suits your personal style and enjoy knocking a simple outfit out of the park!

## You'll Need

- Scraps of leather and vinyl in several different colors
- Scissors
- E-6000 glue
- Fiskars pinking shears
- Large pin
- 3 large pearls
- 3 flathead jewelry pins
- Needle-nose pliers (and wirecutters if the pliers don't have them)
- 2 yards of several different sizes of gold-tone chain
- 10 gold-tone jump rings
- 2 metal end caps

## Here's How

1 Cut your flowers using the patterns on page 367. You will need 17 flowers altogether—five large, five medium, and four small, all in different leathers and vinyls, so that when you assemble them they have variation. Leave out three of the medium flowers to cover the backs.

2 Glue them together with E-6000.

3 Using the pinking shears, cut three small circles. They should be about 1 inch in diameter.

4 Poke a hole in the center of each one with a large pin.

5 Put a pearl on a flathead jewelry pin and poke it through the hole from the front to the back of the flower. Bend the pin so that all the pieces are secured together.

6 Glue a flower on the back of each of the flowers to give it a finished look.

7 Create a three-strand necklace out of your long chain and connect the ends of the chains together with jump rings. Make sure the strands are long enough to fit over your head.

8 To make your tassel, cut a piece of vinyl or leather 2 inches by 4 inches and fringe it with scissors. Glue it inside an end cap.

9 Create chain tassels with five 4-inch pieces of chain on a jump ring.

10 Poke holes on opposite ends of each flower with a large pin and add jump rings. Link them to the chain.

11 Add your chain and leather tassels where you feel they look best.

# BLOOMING WALLET

It's like a corsage, but it has money in it. Seriously, wouldn't you rather have a bouquet full of *money*?

## YOU'LL NEED

- Vinyl or leather scraps
- Scissors
- E-6000 glue
- 24 inches of 18- to 20-gauge wire
- Needle-nose pliers (and wirecutters if the pliers don't have them)
- 8 crystal or pearl beads
- 6 inches of leather, suede, or faux suede lace
- Hot glue gun and glue sticks
- Fiskars pinking shears
- Large pin
- 3 yards of twine to match one of your colors
- Clothespins
- Wallet

## HERE'S HOW

**1** Using the patterns on page 367, with regular scissors, cut out enough flower shapes from your vinyl or leather to create six flowers that have three to four layers of petals each.

**2** Glue the flowers together with E-6000 and let dry.

**3** Cut eight 3-inch pieces of wire. Bend small loops in each wire and attach a crystal or pearl bead to each wire.

**4** Roll your leather or suede lace into a spiral disk (like a cinnamon bun) and hot-glue the end of the disk down so that it holds together. Using pinking shears, cut small circles just a bit bigger than the disk.

**5** Mount the disk on the small pinked circle and then on the flat flowers. Poke a hole through the center with a large pin and push one of the wires with a bead through all of the layers and bend the wire to hold the flower together. Repeat this process for the rest of your flowers.

**6** Cut out eight to ten 8-inch pieces of twine and twist a piece of wire around the center to keep it together, creating a tassel.

**7** Glue the tassels and the flowers on the top of the wallet and let dry. Use clothespins to secure the flowers in place on the wallet while they dry.

**8** Glue a flower over the snap on the front with E-6000 and let dry.

# RAIN FOREST

When I was growing up, my mother and I had an obsession with Cher. I loved her costumes and my mom loved her belly button. In 1985, right after I moved to NYC, I ran into Cher at a salon on the Upper East Side, and she was just lovely to me. My obsession continues, and I've designed this necklace in honor of her. It's very "Gypsys, Tramps & Thieves," with a little "Half-Breed" thrown in for good measure.

## YOU'LL NEED

- 4 pieces of approximately 30-inch gold-tone chains in different sizes plus about 60 inches for the tassels
- Needle-nose pliers (and wirecutters if the pliers don't have them)
- 2 medium gold-tone jump rings
- 1 large gold-tone lobster claw
- ¼ yard of vinyl or leather in any color you like
- Scissors
- 24 inches of 20-gauge wire
- Sewing machine with zigzag stitch
- Lumiere paint in Metallic Copper
- Paintbrush
- Krylon Metallic Gold spray paint
- ½ yard of leather, suede, or faux suede lace (I used orange)
- ½-inch-diameter flat-back acrylic gems (I used orange)
- Hot glue gun and glue sticks
- 15 large gold-tone jump rings (you can make your own by following the instructions in the Crystal Chain-link Necklaces project on page 344)

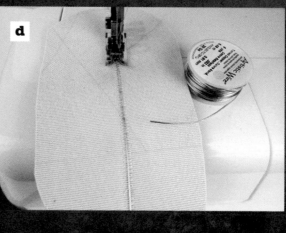

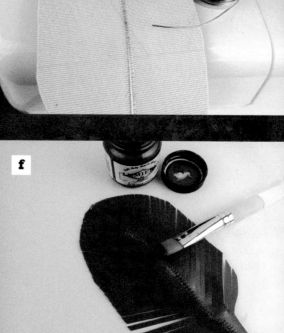

## HeRE's HoW

**1** Cut four pieces of 30-inch-long chain and create a four-strand necklace by connecting them all together with a jump ring at each end and a lobster claw for the closure.

**2** Cut four feathers out of leather or vinyl using the pattern on page 364.

**3** Cut your wire the length of each feather and then zigzag over the wire by placing the wire onto the center of the back of each feather. On the sewing machine, zigzag over it to keep the wire in place.

**4** Fringe the feather with scissors.

**5** Add shimmer to the feathers by painting on the Lumiere copper. Add as much or as little as you want.

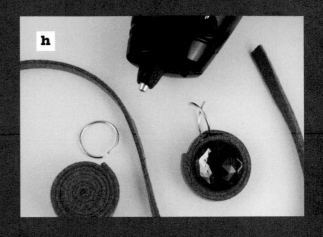

6   Dust the edges of each feather with the Krylon gold spray paint and let dry.

7   Cut seven 6-inch pieces of leather or suede lace and roll them like a cinnamon bun to create leather disks. Secure the ends with hot glue.

8   Hot-glue a gem on each leather disk.

9   Bend the end of each feather to create a loop. Add a large jump ring on the loop and hang at different points along your multistrand necklace. You will have to experiment.

10   Slip a jump ring through your gem-covered leather disks and hang from different points along your necklace.

11   Cut the extra chain into 5-inch pieces and add them to a jump ring to create a tassel. Make two of these and attach them at different points along your necklace.

# WHIRLY BROOCHES

Okay, after creating 150 projects for this book, I just didn't know what else to name these. My brain is whirling around right now and Whirly Brooches was the only thing I could come up with. It happens.

## YoU'LL NeED

- ◆ Leather or vinyl scraps in two matching colors
- ◆ Scissors
- ◆ E-6000 glue
- ◆ Clothespins
- ◆ Lumiere acrylic paints in pearl turquoise, green, and gold
- ◆ Small paintbrush
- ◆ Hot glue gun and glue sticks
- ◆ Pearls in different sizes
- ◆ Pin backs for as many brooches as you want to make
- ◆ 14 inches of leather, suede, or faux suede lace (for the Leafy Brooch)
- ◆ Toothpicks

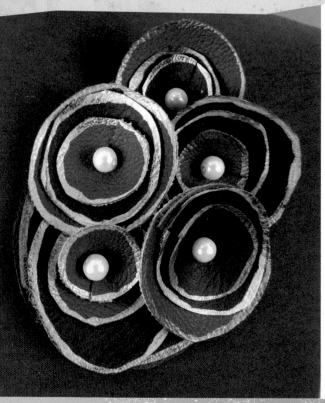

## HeRE's HoW

**1** For each brooch, cut 5 sets of circles (small, medium, and large) in different colors of vinyl or leather, starting at 3 inches in diameter and getting smaller.

**2** Cut to the center of each circle, overlapping about ¼ inch where you cut to create an almost flat cone shape. Secure with a dab of E-6000 and a clothespin until it dries.

**3** Paint the edges of each circle with the Lumiere paint and let dry.

**4** Glue sets of three circles together with E-6000 and let dry.

**5** Cut out an oval 4 inches by 3 inches from your vinyl or leather. Glue several flowers on with E-6000 and let dry.

**6** Glue a pearl in the center of each flower with E-6000.

**7** Glue a pin back to the brooch with E-6000 and let dry.

## FOR THE LEAFY BROOCH

**1** Cut a set of four circles, the largest being 3½ inches in diameter and getting smaller.

**2** Cut to the center of each circle, overlapping about ¼ inch where you cut to create a very flat cone shape. Secure with a dab of E-6000 glue and a clothespin until it dries.

**3** Paint the edges of each circle with turquoise and gold Lumiere paint.

**4** Create spiral disks by rolling up the leather or suede lace (like a cinnamon bun). Secure the edge with hot glue.

**5** Cut five leaves about 2 inches long by 1 inch wide from your vinyl or leather.

**6** Add a dab of hot glue at the end of each leaf and pinch until it dries. This will give it some dimension.

**7** Paint the edges of each leaf green and gold.

**8** Cut an oval about 3 inches by 2 inches from your vinyl or leather and glue on your large circular flower with E-6000.

**9** Using a tiny dab of hot glue, position the leaves under the big flower. With dabs of E-6000 on a toothpick, glue them in place.

**10** Glue on your leather disks and then the pearls with more E-6000 and let dry.

**11** Flip the piece over and glue your pin back on with E-6000.

# COMING AND GOING IN CIRCLES

My mom once told me that people who draw circles are crazy. She told me this as I was drawing circles. Even though most people who know me would agree that I am a little off my rocker, I still love every kind of circle, and they look terrific on this bag and wallet. It's a great way to revamp an old purse or spruce up a cheapo wallet. With just a few supplies, you can take this technique and apply it to just about anything.

## YOU'LL NEED

- ¼ yard of six different colors of vinyl or leather
- 3 circle patterns of different sizes (glasses or stencils)
- Fiskars pinking shears
- E-6000 glue
- Old purse and wallet

## FOR THE WALLET

- Above, plus flat-back acrylic gems

## FOR THE PURSE DANGLE AND KEY CHAIN

- Flat-back acrylic gems
- Large pin
- 2 jump rings
- 8 inches of medium silver- or gold-tone chain
- Needle-nose pliers
  (and wirecutters if the pliers don't have them)
- Hot glue gun and glue sticks

## HERE'S HOW

**1** Trace six of each size of circle (small, medium, and large) on the back of your vinyl or leather.

**2** Cut them out with pinking shears.

**3** Experiment with color combinations on your bag before you start gluing and figure out how many you'll need for the project. Depending on the size of the bag, you may have to cut more.

**4** Glue the circles together, layering one on top of another from smallest to largest, using the E-6000 first before putting them on the bag.

**5** Glue the finished circles to the bag and lay something heavy over it so they dry in place and flat.

## FOR THE WALLET

*You will need only two different-size circles (small and medium) for the wallet in several different colors of vinyl. My circles were about 1½ inches and 1 inch in diameter.*

**1** Cut out your circles using pinking shears.

**2** Figure out your color combinations and how they will look on your wallet.

**3** Layer your circles and glue them together first before you put them on the wallet and before you add the gems.

**4** Glue the circles on the wallet and lay a book on top so they dry flat and in place.

**5** When dry, add a gem to the center of each circle with more E-6000 and let dry.

## FOR THE KEY CHAIN OR PURSE DANGLE

**1** Glue together two sets of three circles, adding a flat-back gem to the center of each set, and let dry.

**2** Glue the finished circles back to back with hot glue.

**3** Poke a hole on the edge of the two-sided circle with a large pin and push a jump ring through the hole.

**4** Add the chain and close the jump ring.

# GARDEN PARTY

When I was growing up, my brothers and I would spend Saturdays with our dad at work. We loved watching him fix cars and do upholstery in the back of his shop. He was good at it, too—both the upholstery *and* fixing cars. As you can guess, I was always in the sewing part of the shop playing with vinyl and my brothers were usually outside getting dirty. I used to get the most amazing scraps of vinyl to play with, and this is where my obsession with vinyl flowers began. Change the colors of this project to fit your own taste and style.

## YOU'LL NEED

- Scraps of vinyl or leather in different colors
- Scissors
- E-6000 glue
- Clothespins
- Lumiere pearl turquoise acrylic paint
- 21 inches of 18-gauge wire
- Needle-nose pliers (and wirecutters if the pliers don't have them)
- Several crystal beads
- Several pearl beads
- 3 yards of blue leather, suede, or faux suede lace
- Hot glue gun and glue sticks
- Fiskars pinking shears
- Large pin
- 4 silver-tone jump rings
- 16 inches medium silver-tone chain
- 1 silver-tone lobster claw closure

## HERE'S HOW

1. Using the patterns on page 367, cut out enough flower shapes with regular scissors to create six flowers with three to four layers of petals each.

2. Cut to the center of the curved-edge flowers, overlapping the edges where you cut about ¼ inch so it creates a very flat cone shape, and glue them together with E-6000. This will make them look three-dimensional. Hold in place with clothespins while they dry.

3. Paint the edges with the pearl turquoise acrylic paint and let dry.

4. Glue the flowers together with E-6000 glue and let dry.

5. Cut the wire into seven 3-inch pieces. Bend small loops in the wire, and put a crystal or pearl bead on each one.

6. Cut five pieces of the leather or suede lace into 6-inch pieces. Roll each into a spiral disk (like a cinnamon bun) and hot-glue the end of the lace to the disk so that it holds together. Make five of these.

7. With pinking shears, cut five small circles just a bit bigger than the disks.

8. Mount the disks on the small pinked circles and then on the flat flowers and put a wire with a bead through all of the layers. Bend the wire on the back of the flower to secure the piece.

9. Cut out a base piece of vinyl or leather in the size you want that will accommodate all your flowers.

10. Cut out two pieces of vinyl or leather about 4 inches wide by 6 inches long and fringe them.

11. Cut several pieces of the leather or suede lace about 8 inches long.

12. Glue the fringe and leather strips on the base and the flowers over the top of the fringed pieces with E-6000 and let dry.

13. Poke a hole in the sides of your flower piece with a large pin and add a jump ring on each side. Cut your chain into two 8-inch pieces and attach to jump ring on each side.

14. Add jump rings to the ends of the chain and a lobster claw for the closure.

# WOODN'T IT BE LOVELY?

s I'm writing this, I realize that everything I know about wood, I learned from my grandfather. He had a tiny shed behind his house filled with tools perfectly mounted on pegboard. He was a skilled carpenter who loved to fish and was rarely without his Old Fart baseball cap. For Christmas one year I asked him for wood blocks and got exactly what I wished for— TONS of them. Not just a small set, but literally hundreds in all different shapes and sizes— they were beautiful. Slowly over time I learned how to use the band saw, the jigsaw, and finally, when I was old enough, the chop saw. I think about him every time I make a project with wood, even with the most basic tools.

# BLUE BIRD BANGLE

The first person I showed this to thought I was out of my mind. The second and third people who saw it fell madly in love with it. I'm no longer friends with the first person, who clearly has no taste. This is by far my favorite project in this book. I have no idea why it speaks to me so much, it just does.

## YOU'LL NEED

- ¼-inch birch plywood (4 inches by 4 inches)
- Jigsaw with fine blade or band saw (or, better yet, someone to cut for you!)
- Fine sandpaper
- Minwax Express Color in Indigo
- Minwax Polycrylic clear coat
- Small paintbrushes
- Cast of bird head (see page 232 for casting instructions and materials)
- Krylon spray paint in Metallic Gold
- E-6000 glue

## HeRE's HoW

1 Using the patterns on page 371, cut out your bangle from the birch plywood. Make sure that the opening is wide enough for your wrist but not so big that it falls off.

2 Sand it nice and smooth.

3 Stain it with Minwax Express Color using a small brush. If you use too much, wipe off the excess with a rag so that the wood grain still shows through.

4 Brush Minwax Polycrylic on both sides and let dry.

5 Make a mold and cast your bird head. (See instructions and materials on page 232). When dry, spray with the metallic gold.

6 Glue your bird head on the pointed part of the bangle with E-6000 and let dry.

# MAGICAL MIRROR

Mirror, mirror on the wall, who is the *blingiest* of them all? Isn't it obvious?
Add some sparkle to your morning routine with this crystal-trimmed mirror, and just
like in the toothpaste commercials, you'll see a tiny sparkle on your front teeth every
time you look at yourself!

## YOU'LL NEED

- 1 large wood frame with glass front
- Sandpaper
- Minwax water-base wood stain in Black
- Lumiere metallic paint in Pewter
- Rags
- Paintbrush
- Enough crystal chain to circle the frame twice
- Needle-nose pliers (and wirecutters if the pliers don't have them)
- E-6000 glue
- Toothpicks
- Krylon Looking Glass paint
- Minwax Polycrylic clear coat

## HERE'S HOW

1. Sand off any finish that might be on your frame so it will stain evenly.

2. Apply a coat of the Minwax stain and rub it into the wood so that you can see the wood grain.

3. With a rag, apply a small amount of the Lumiere

Pewter on top to give it some shimmer.

**4** With a paintbrush, coat your frame with Minwax Polycrylic clear coat and let dry.

**5** Measure your frame and cut enough crystal chain to encircle the frame twice. Carefully glue crystal chain around the outside and inside edges of the frame using E-6000 on a toothpick.

**6** Spray one side of the glass with the Krylon Looking Glass paint.

**7** Frame the glass (which is now a mirror) in the frame and hang.

# NATURE'S BLING NECKLACE

Sometimes I'm in awe of how beautiful nature can be . . . and how cruel! The very branch that I've used to make this necklace was the one that crashed down on my new car and dented it! In an effort to turn lemons into lemonade, I cut up the branches and made these beautiful little wooden disks. Okay, fine, I had my friend Josh cut them up.

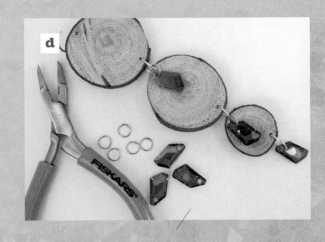

## YOU'LL NEED

- Branches of various sizes (about 1 to 2 inches in diameter)
- Jigsaw or band saw or someone to cut the branches for you
- Minwax Polycrylic clear coat
- Rags
- Paintbrush
- Drill with ¹⁄₁₆-inch drill bit
- 20 large gold-tone jump rings
- 16 inches of thick gold-tone chain (I like gold for this project with the warm tones of the wood)
- 19 crystal beads or drops (mine were Swarovski, but you can use almost anything)
- 14 small gold-tone jump rings
- 1 gold-tone lobster claw closure
- Needle-nose pliers (and wirecutters if the pliers don't have them)
- Sandpaper

## HERE'S HOW

1. Cut 14 disks of wood of various sizes from your branches. As you can see, mine ranged from large to small. Cut tons of extras just in case you want to make another project, like the bag on page 44.

2. With a paintbrush, coat each disk with Minwax Polycrylic to give it a nice finish. Don't forget, it will last much longer this way!

3. Drill two small holes on opposite ends of each disk.

4. Lay out your design with four disks in the center, three on either side of those disks, and two on either side of those.

5. Use the larger jump rings to attach your longest strand of wood disks to each other and to the gold chain at the exact center.

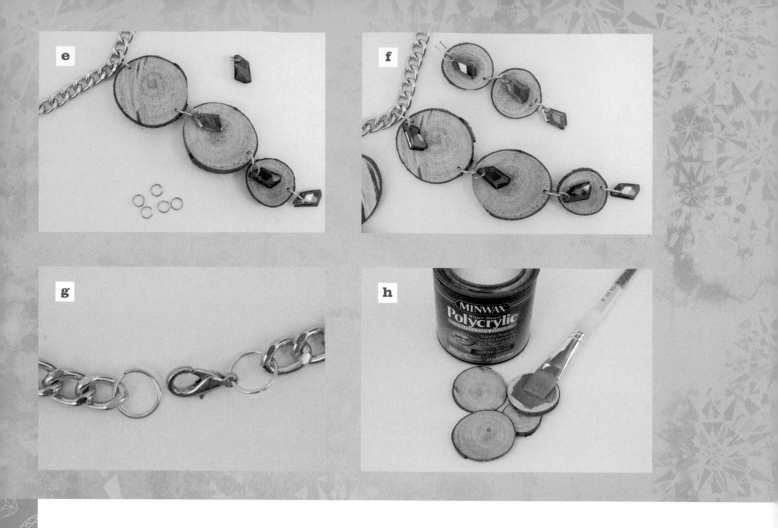

6  Attach your other strands to the chain in an even
   pattern as shown in photo f.

7  Using the smaller jump rings, add a crystal to
   the front of each disk of wood and to the bottom
   of each strand of wood disks.

8  Add small jump rings to the ends of your chain
   and a lobster claw for the closure.

# SOUTHWEST STYLE

I have always loved the bold jewelry of the Southwest. The huge chunks of turquoise and leather pieces that women wear—even in the most casual way—are stunning. Every time I go to New Mexico or back home to southern Colorado, I'm reminded that there are hundreds, perhaps thousands, of different distinct regional styles all over the world. How cool is that!

## YOU'LL NEED

- Chunk of paper turquoise (see page 74), Glass Gem (see page 141) or stone you have and want to feature
- ¼-inch birch plywood (4 inches by 4 inches)
- Jigsaw with fine blade or band saw or someone to cut the wood for you
- Sandpaper
- Drill with ³⁄₁₆-inch drill bit
- Minwax Express Color in crimson
- Paintbrush
- Rags
- Minwax Polycrylic clear coat
- 20-gauge wire
- Needle-nose pliers (and wirecutters if the pliers don't have them)
- Lobster claw closure
- 4 feet each of three colors of leather, suede, or faux suede lace (I used orange, burgundy, and brown)
- E-6000 glue

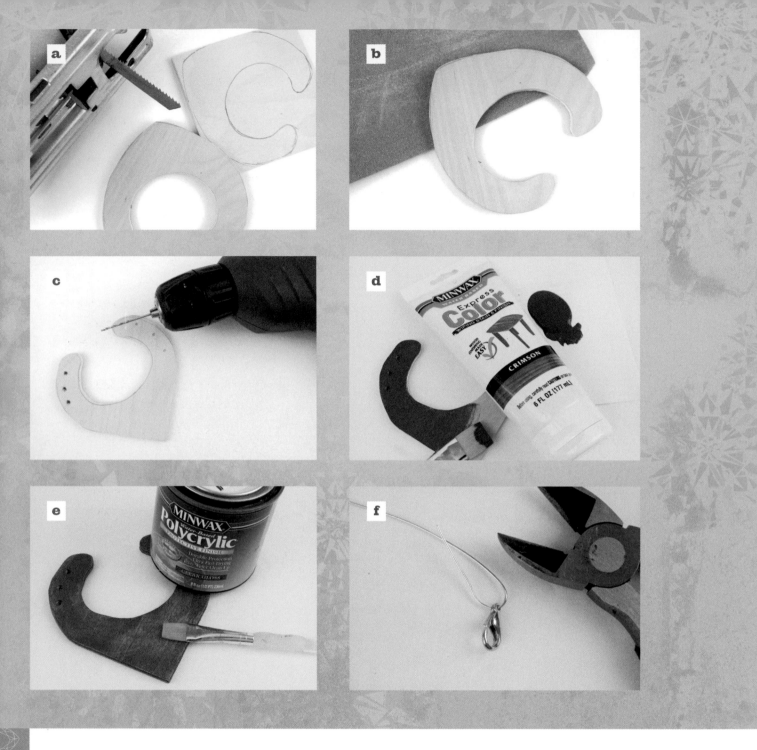

## HeRE's How

1. Cut your wood centerpiece, using the pattern on page 368.

2. Sand it and wipe off the dust.

3. Drill three holes on each side about ½ inch apart and clean the drill holes with sand paper.

4. Paint on the Minwax Color Express. Wipe off the excess so the wood grain shows through.

5. With a paintbrush, clear-coat your wood centerpiece with the Minwax Polycrylic.

6. Cut 6 inches of wire, thread on a lobster claw, and twist it into a loop toward the end. The twist should be about ¾ inch long.

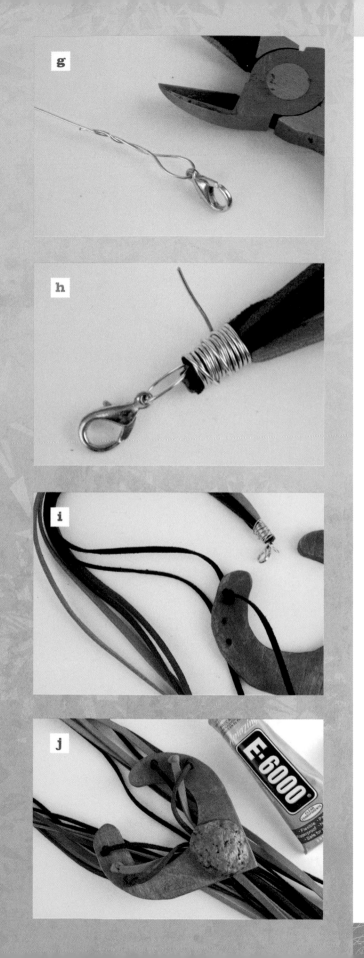

7. Cut all of your leather and suede laces in half.

8. Take the ends of the six strands and tuck in the wire loop so that it's peeking out at the top. Tightly wrap the wire strands together with extra wire.

9. Do the same on the other end of the six strands, but without the lobster claw.

10. Thread three of the strands through the back of the holes on each side of your wood centerpiece and knot in the front where you want them to stay.

11. Tuck the excess laces behind the wood piece as shown in photo j.

12. Knot some of the ends of the leather strips.

13. Glue a big piece of paper turquoise to the center of the wood piece with E-6000 and let dry.

**Suggestion:**
You could use any stone for this project. Try using a fused glass piece from the Glass-terpiece chapter.

# WOOD AND GOLD LEAF CUFFS

Glints of gold leaf make these wood cuffs look even richer. They are simple and catch the light just beautifully. I know you'll enjoy wearing them as much as you'll have fun making them. This would be a perfect project for you and your other half to do together, too.

## YOU'LL NEED

- ¼-inch birch plywood (4 inches by 4 inches for each cuff)
- Jigsaw with fine blade or band saw or someone to cut the wood for you
- Sandpaper
- Minwax Express Color wiping stains
- Rags
- Paintbrushes
- Krylon spray adhesive
- Painter's tape or masking tape and scrap paper
- Gold leaf
- 1-inch flat brush
- Minwax Polycrylic clear coat

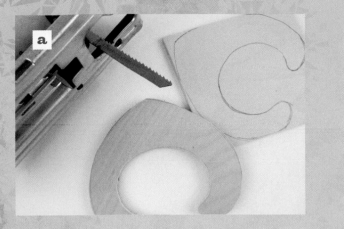

## HeRE's HoW

1. Cut your wood cuffs, using the patterns on page 370.

2. Sand them with fine sandpaper and wipe off the dust.

3. Paint them with the Minwax Express Color. Make sure to wipe off excess stain so that you can see the wood grain underneath. I think this contributes to the beauty of this project.

4. Mask off some areas of your wood cuff with paper and tape. The exposed parts will be gilded.

5. Spray with the spray adhesive.

6. Carefully apply gold leaf onto the adhesive areas and let dry.

7. Wipe away any excess gold leaf with your brush.

8. Apply three thin coats of Minwax Polycrylic with a paintbrush and let dry for about 15 minutes in between each coat.

# NATURE'S BLING BAG

Tree-mendous! Woodsy! A great way to "branch" out your personal style. Earthy-crunchy couture. Too many things are whirling through my head right now, "woodn't" you know it!

## YOU'LL NEED

- Old leather bag (medium size) in need of some nature love
- Branches of various sizes (about ½ to 2 inches in diameter)
- Jigsaw with wood blade or band saw or someone to cut the branches for you
- Minwax Polycrylic clear coat
- Wood-burning tool
- 20 small flat-back crystals or gems (mine were Swarovski, but you could use almost anything)
- E-6000 glue

## HERE'S HOW

1. Cut 80 to 90 disks of various sizes from your branches. As you can see, mine range from ½ inch to 2 inches in diameter. Cut tons of extras just in case you want to make another project, like the necklace on page 36.

2. On some of the larger disks, burn a starburst design with your wood-burning tool as shown in photo c.

3. Coat each disk with Minwax Polycrylic to give it a nice finish. Don't forget, it will last much longer this way!

4. Lay out your design on your bag so you know about how you want it to look.

5  Glue a gem in the center of the starburst design with a tiny dab of E-6000.

6  Glue each disk on your bag—and along the handle, too, if you like—with generous amounts of E-6000 and let dry.

*Hint:*
**Sometimes it helps if you take a digital photo of your work before you start to glue it down.**

**W**hat is it about tiaras and crowns that make us feel young again? There are two little girls on my block who are going through the princess phase right now, and every morning when I'm running up and down the stairs for exercise I see tiny versions of Glenda the Good Witch headed for school. Am I jealous? Hell, yes, I am! Why can't I wear a crown and sparkly shoes? I say, relive your princess phase and make some of these for your next party! Sending out a special thanks to my friend Corinne from Threadbanger for the inspiration for these projects.

# GLENDA THE GOOD WITCH CROWN

Nothing says "Glenda the Good Witch" like a crown full of sparkly stars. I'm not saying you'll find the Wizard, but I *am* saying you'll be the life of the party. Just a warning: Beware of flying monkeys!

## YOU'LL NEED

- 20-gauge wire
- Needle-nose pliers (and wirecutters if the pliers don't have them)
- Plastic hairband
- Krylon spray paint in Purple or Pink
- Card stock in several shades of pink and purple
- Fiskars star punch (see Resource Guide)
- Flat-back acrylic gems
- Hot glue gun and glue sticks
- Krylon Glitter Blast spray paint in pink

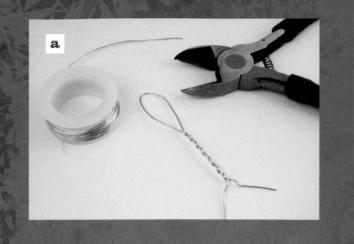

## HeRE's HoW

**1** Cut seven 10-inch pieces of wire.

**2** Loop each wire in half and twist it, leaving 2 inches at the bottom.

**3** Wrap those ends around the plastic hairband, with one end wrapping in one direction and the other end in the opposite direction, starting in the center and working your way out.

**4** Continue until you have all seven pieces of wire on your crown in a triangular shape as shown in photo c.

**5** Spray-paint the entire wire crown in Purple or Pink and let dry.

**6** Punch out your stars from the different-colored card stocks. I'd start with about 30, and if you need more, keep punching.

**7** Hot-glue them to the wire wrapping and make sure they are secure. Work from the inside of the crown if you need to and cover up the hot glue with more stars on the inside of the crown.

**8** Add acrylic gems wherever you like with a little more hot glue.

**9** Lightly spray the entire crown with a little pink Krylon Glitter Blast to give it sparkle.

# THE BUTTERFLY FAIRY CROWN

From what I understand, if you possess the Butterfly Fairy's crown, you have her powers as well. At least this is what my niece told me, and she believes it wholeheartedly. Fortunately for me, I have access to this very crown. All I had to do was point my glue gun at the Butterfly Fairy, and she gave it up without a fight. It's a big glue gun, and I can be pretty relentless when trying to find the perfect gift for my niece!

## YOU'LL NEED

- 3 yards of 20-gauge wire
- Needle-nose pliers (and wirecutters if the pliers don't have them)
- Plastic hairband
- Silver Krylon spray paint
- 12 wire and nylon butterflies in various colors and sizes (most craft and party stores carry these)
- Hot glue gun and glue sticks
- ½-inch and ¾-inch-diameter flat-back acrylic gems (about 10 in all)

## HERE'S HOW

1. Cut nine 10-inch pieces of wire.

2. Loop seven pieces of the wire in half and twist each piece, leaving 2 inches at the bottom.

3. Wrap those ends around the plastic hairband, with one end wrapping in one direction and the other end in the opposite direction, starting in the center and working your way out.

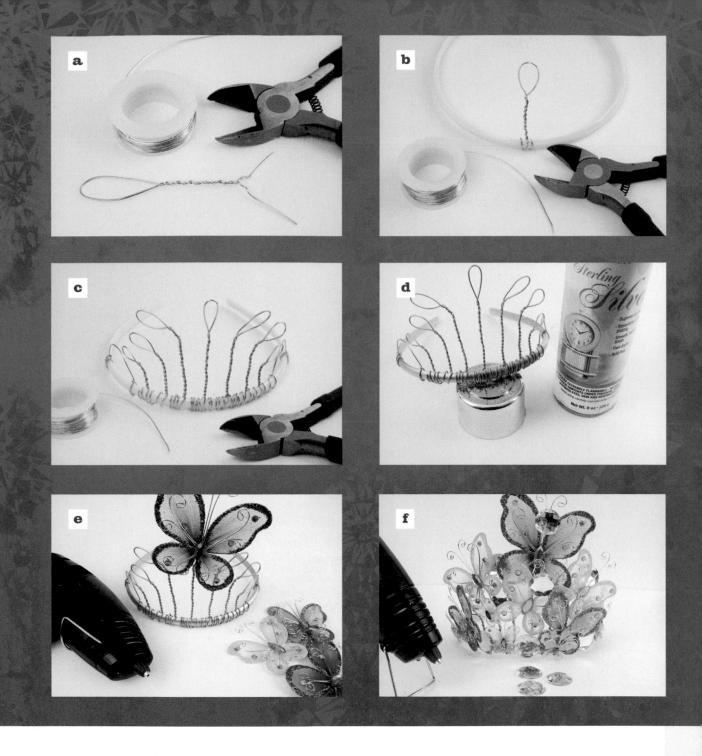

**4** Continue until you have wrapped seven pieces of wire on your crown, bent to descend in height from the center.

**5** Take the remaining two pieces of wire and make a semicircle on each side by bending the wire around the hairband.

**6** Spray-paint the crown silver and let dry.

**7** Hot-glue the butterflies to the wire and make sure they are secure.

**8** Add acrylic gems wherever you like with a little more hot glue to fill in any empty spaces.

# GOLD KRYLON KROWN

I'm just going to admit it. I wore this around the house for an entire day and loved every minute of it. Even the mail lady commented on my fashion statement, saying it made me look regal. The fact is that wearing a crown makes you feel amazing. Trust me on this.

## YOU'LL NEED

- 3 yards of 20-gauge wire
- Needle-nose pliers
  (and wirecutters if the pliers don't have them)
- 130 plastic faceted beads
- 1 plastic hairband
- Krylon gray primer
- Krylon gold metallic paint
- 5 hot pink flat-back gems
  (¾-inch-diameter)
- E-6000 glue
- Toothpicks

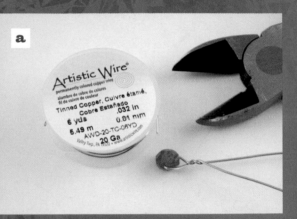

*Hint:*

Use crystal beads in one color if you don't want to spray-paint this!

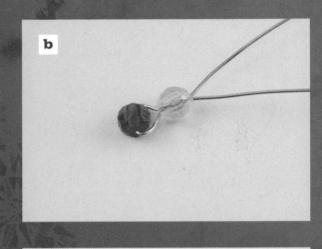

## HERE'S HOW

1. Cut five 12-inch pieces of wire,.

2. Center a bead on one wire and twist twice just under the bead.

3. Place a bead over both wires and position it underneath the first bead to cover the twisted wire.

4. Separate the wires and add five beads to each wire and twist again to form a loop of beads as shown in photo c.

5. Add another bead over both wires to cover the twisted wire.

6. Separate the wires and add four beads to each wire and twist again.

7. Add another bead to cover the twist.

8. Bend the excess wire around the exact center of the hairband and wrap one end in one direction, the other end in the opposite direction, starting in the center and working your way out.

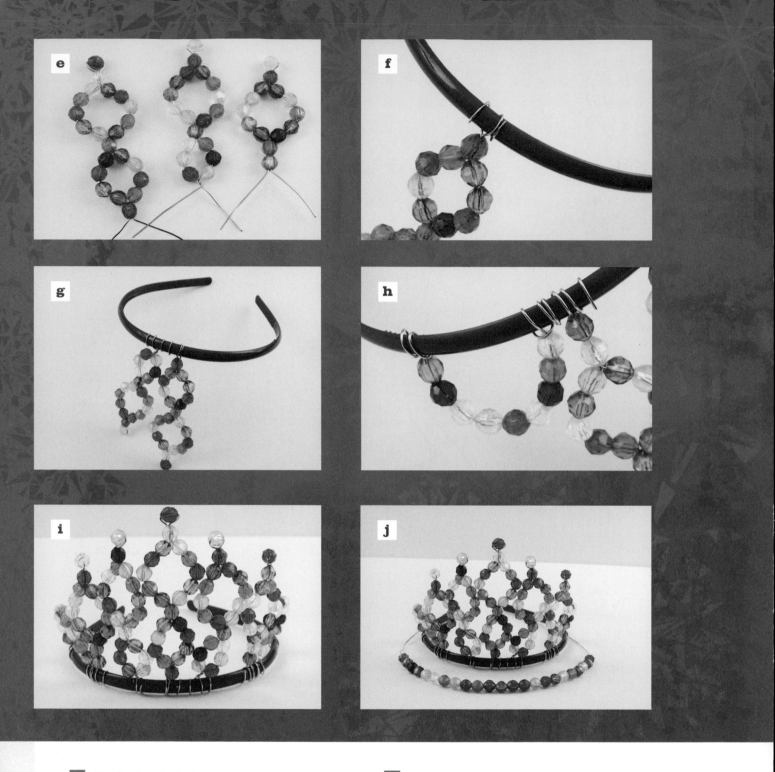

9  For the beaded pieces on each side of your middle piece, repeat the above process twice using only three beads for step 6 and skipping steps 7 and 8.

10  For the next two beaded pieces repeat steps 1 through 4, but add two beads for step 5 as shown in photo e.

11  Add the beaded pieces to your hairband in descending order from tallest to shortest.

12  Cut two pieces of wire 7 inches long and string nine beads on each.

13  Make a semicircle and attach each end of the wire for the last beaded wire piece on your hairband as shown in photo h.

**14** Take another 12-inch piece of wire and string approximately 22 beads on it. This strand of beads will cover the wire wrapping on the hairband.

**15** With the beads across the hairband, wrap the excess ends of the wire around the hairband where your beads end on each side. DON'T WORRY: Right now the beads will not reach from end to end, and there will be extra exposed wire between them. You will need this extra space for the next step.

**16** Cut an 18-inch piece of wire and wrap it around the hairband in between each bead to keep them in place.

**17** Form your beaded pieces into a crown shape (in case it got bent while adding your last row of beads).

**18** Spray-paint your crown with the Krylon gray primer and let dry.

**19** Spray-paint the crown with the metallic gold and let dry.

**20** With dabs of E-6000 on a toothpick, carefully add your hot pink gems and let dry.

# QUEEN OF THE NIGHT

Some girls just aren't pink and sparkly. I discovered this while hanging out with my friend Jenny, who prefers leather boots to stiletto heels. When she got married to her husband, John, we were all a little surprised for many reasons. Jenny is the kind of girl you call when you have a flat tire or need your washing machine fixed. She's invaluable. For her bachelorette party, I had to make her this crown, because it just fit her style. Anything with color would have ended up in the back of her truck, hidden in her toolbox. We love you, Jenny!

## YOU'LL NEED

- 3 yards of 20-gauge wire
- Needle-nose pliers (and wirecutters if the pliers don't have them)
- 1 plastic hairband
- 130 plastic faceted beads
- Krylon gray primer
- Krylon Fusion for Plastics spray paint in Black
- 10 flat-back acrylic gems in either Black or a color
- E-6000 glue
- Toothpicks

*Hint:*
For process shots of this project, check out the GOLD KRYLON KROWN craft—the steps are almost identical until the end!

## HERE'S HOW

Follow the same process shots and steps #1–18 from the Gold Krylon Krown project on pages 52–55.

**19** Spray-paint the entire crown with the black high-gloss spray paint and let dry.

**20** With dabs of E-6000 on a toothpick, carefully add your acrylic gems, and let dry.

# LACE AND RESIN CROWN

It was like the sky opened up when I figured out how to make this lace crown work! I had been trying to do this for a while, but I just couldn't figure it out. Finally, my friend Jen sent me some ICE Resin (the best two-step resin on the market), so I tried it. Once the lace dried, a whole new world of crafting appeared right in front of me. (By the way, this might be PERFECT for a bride!)

- Thick lace
- Hot glue gun and glue sticks
- 2 large pieces of cardboard
- 2 feet of wax paper
- Newspaper
- Several straight pins
- ICE Resin
- Disposable paintbrush
- Rubber or plastic gloves
- Jacquard Lumiere Metallic paint in Silver
- *Optional:* 2 small hair combs and E-6000 glue

## HeRE's HoW

1. Design your crown. Decide what shape you prefer, and write down the measurements for how large the crown should be.

2. With tiny dabs of hot glue, glue your lace pieces together in the shape of the crown on a flat surface.

3. Carefully make a 10-inch-long tube with a piece of cardboard that will fit around your head comfortably.

4. Cover the tube with wax paper and hot-glue it to the tube so it stays in place.

5. Create two round tubes of newspaper and hot-glue them to the cardboard, parallel to one another, about 2 inches apart. This is what you will rest your tube on while the resin is drying.

6. Carefully pin your lace on top of the tube so that it takes the shape of the tube.. You can use tiny dabs of hot glue, too, but it might not stick to the wax paper. Still, give it a try.

7. Once your lace crown is in place, if you need to, review the instructions on the ICE Resin and my tips on page 232. Mix your resin outside using gloves. The fumes from resin can be harsh and you will need to work in a well-ventilated area. You will need about ¼ cup for this project.

8. With your stiff paintbrush, neatly paint the resin on the lace, soaking every part of it as you go. Make sure not to miss a spot.

9. Let your project dry overnight on wax paper in a room or area of the house you don't use (it will dry a little faster if you put it under a desk lamp). Remove it from the cardboard tubes.

10. Paint the entire lace crown with the Jacquard Lumiere metallic paint and let dry.

11. Pin in place with bobby pins, or you can glue some combs in the back to keep it secure.

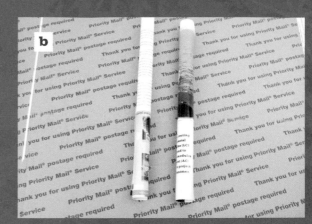

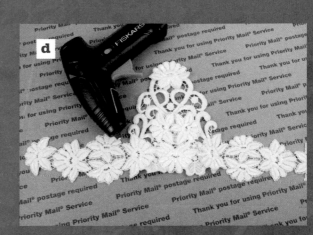

59

# THE QUEEN'S PEARL TIARA

I'm not really a betting person, but I'd bet a thousand bucks that the Queen of England runs around the house in one of these! When I finished making this crown, I put it on, bossed my assistant around for an hour, and loved every minute of it. Can you imagine if it really *were* her crown?! God save the Queen!

## YOU'LL NEED

- 3 yards of 20-gauge wire
- 1 pink plastic hairband
- 40 large pearls
- 130 small pearls
- Needle-nose pliers (and wirecutters if the pliers don't have them)

## HERE'S HOW

**1** Cut five 12-inch pieces of wire.

**2** Center a pearl on one piece of wire and twist twice just under the bead.

**3** Separate the wires and add five small pearls to each wire and twist again to form a loop of pearls.

**4** Add another pearl over both wires to cover the twisted wire.

**5** Separate the wires and add five more small pearls to each wire and twist again.

**6** Add another bead to cover the twist.

**7** Bend the excess wire around the exact center of the hairband. Wrap those ends around the plastic hairband, with one end wrapping in one direction and the other end in the opposite direction, starting in the center and working your way out.

**8** For the shorter pieces on each side of your middle piece, repeat the above process but don't add your bottom large pearl.

**9** For the next two beaded pieces repeat steps 1 through 4 and then add two small, two large, and two more small pearls, as shown in photo f.

**10** Take another 12-inch piece of wire and string approximately 20 pearls on it. This will be the strand of pearls that covers the wire wrapping on the hairband.

**11** With the pearls across the hairband, wrap the excess ends of the wire around the hairband where your pearls end on each side. DON'T WORRY: Right now the pearls will not reach from end to end and there will be extra exposed wire between them. You will need this extra space for the next step.

**12** Cut an 18-inch piece of wire and wrap it around the hairband in between each bead to keep them in place.

**13** Adjust the fit of your beaded pieces on your crown, in case it got bent while adding your last row of pearls.

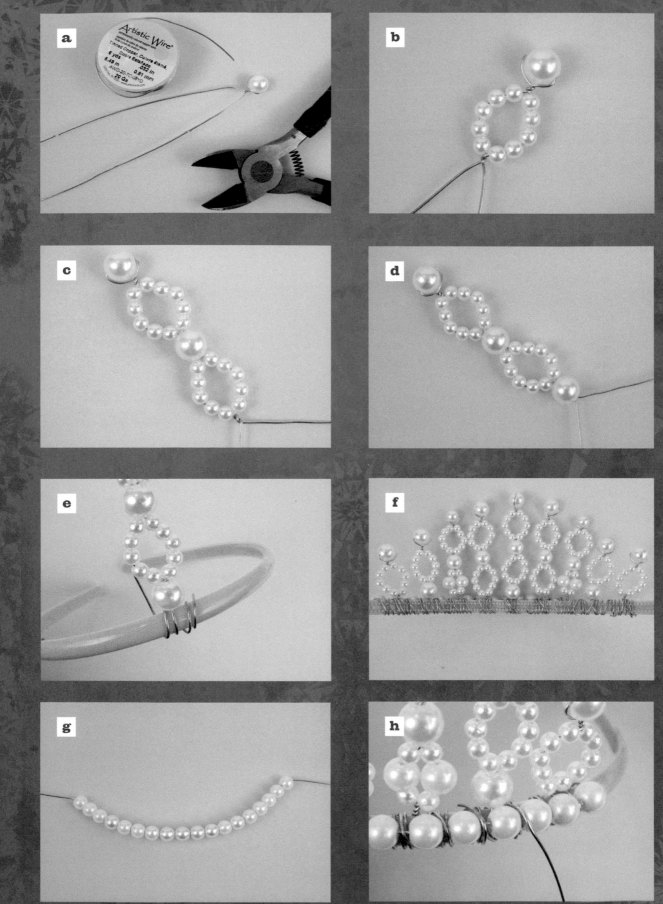

# HaRD As LaCe

I like seeing jewelry made of lace, but I wanted to figure how to make it last forever. I began experimenting and eventually asked myself, what if I soaked it in ICE Resin? (See page 232 and Resource Guide.) The results were amazing. At first I let the pieces dry on plain cardboard and couldn't get them to come off . . . and then I realized that resin won't stick to wax paper. Once I had my technique down, the game was ON!

# LACE AND RESIN CAMEO NECKLACE

I had a drama teacher in high school named Mrs. Mayhew, and she was fantastic. So full of life! What a dresser, too! She moved to our little town from a larger—and much more sophisticated—city, and you could tell. I thought she was just fantastic. I remember her wearing lace dresses and cameos at her neck, and this piece made me think of her and her wonderful antique style.

## You'll Need

- Lace pieces
- Image for the cameo (see page 375)
- Small tin oval (cut your own from aluminum flashing to fit your cameo)
- Elmer's Glue-All
- Wax paper
- Piece of cardboard big enough to accommodate necklace while it dries
- ICE Resin
- Disposable paintbrush
- Lumiere metallic silver and turquoise paints
- Small paintbrush (for the paints)
- E-6000 glue
- 20 silver-tone jump rings
- Large pin
- 1 yard of silver-tone chain
- Needle-nose pliers (and wirecutters if the pliers don't have them)
- 11 crystal beads (any kind of bead that matches will do)
- 1 lobster claw closure
- Rubber or plastic gloves

## HeRE's HoW

**1** Figure out the design and size you want for your necklace and then cut the lace pieces you'll need. Cut some extra, just in case you change your mind or want to make earrings.

**2** Create the cameo by gluing the image you've chosen on top of your tin oval with Elmer's glue.

**3** Place some wax paper on a piece of cardboard and lay your lace pieces and cameo on top.

**4** If you need to, review my instructions and tips for using the ICE Resin on page 232. Mix your resin outside using gloves. The fumes from resin can be harsh and you will need to work in a well-ventilated area. Pour resin on top of your cameo and paint your lace pieces with an old paintbrush until every piece is soaked. Let dry overnight on wax paper and in a room or area of your house that you don't use.

*Hint:*
They will dry more quickly if you leave them under a desk lamp.

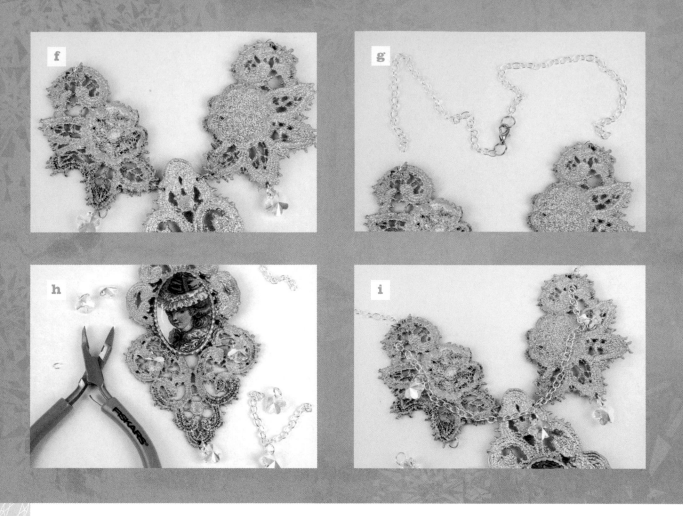

**5** When the lace pieces are dry, paint them with Lumiere metallic silver paint and edge it with the turquoise. (Remember, you can choose any colors you want here.)

**6** With the E-6000, glue your cameo on top of the painted pieces.

**7** Add jump rings to hold your lace pieces together. If you're having a hard time finding a hole, just poke a large pin through the lace to create one.

**8** Add crystals or beads with jump rings off the edges of the piece. ( Place them wherever you see fit!)

**9** Add equal lengths of chain to each side of your lace piece (depending on how long you want your necklace) and attach the chains to the ends of the lace with jump rings to create the necklace. Add jump rings and a lobster claw for the closure.

**10** Dangle more lengths of chain with crystals from the jump ring where your necklace chain starts.

# MARIE ANTOINETTE CAMEO BROOCH

You could use any image for this brooch—it depends on your taste. You could also use this project as the focal point for a choker or necklace. I call it the Marie Antoinette Cameo Brooch because the illustration I used was from that time period. Hey, you could name it the Fido Brooch or the Antique Photo of my Grandma Brooch. Your call!

## YOU'LL NEED

- Lace pieces
- Image for the cameo (see page 375)
- Cameo-size tin oval (cut your own from aluminum flashing)
- Elmer's Glue-All
- Wax paper
- Piece of cardboard big enough to accommodate piece while it dries
- ICE Resin (see page 232)
- Disposable paintbrush
- 8 inches of ¾-inch ribbon
- Hot glue gun and glue sticks
- Feathers
- Pearls
- Large flat-back gem
- Pin back
- E-6000 glue
- Rubber or plastic gloves

## HERE'S HOW

1. Cut the lace pieces you want to use for the backing of the brooch.

2. Create your cameo by gluing the image you've chosen on top of your tin oval with Elmer's glue.

3. Place some wax paper on a piece of cardboard and lay your lace pieces and cameo on top.

4. Mix your resin outside using gloves. The fumes from resin can be harsh and you will need to work in a well-ventilated area. Pour resin on top of your cameo and paint your lace pieces with the resin until every piece is soaked through. Let them dry overnight.

*Hint:*
They will dry more quickly if you leave them under a desk lamp.

**5** Create a small bow with your ribbon.

**6** When your pieces are dry and hard, hot-glue feathers to the back of the cameo and the entire piece on top of the resin-coated lace.

**7** Hot-glue your ribbon bow, pearls, and gem to your piece and let dry.

**8** Finish your brooch by gluing on the pin back with E-6000 and let dry.

# LACE IN PLACE

I'm not sure about you, but when I go into a trim store I start to hyperventilate. To me, it's like magic by the yard. Need to dress up an old pillow? Head to the trim store. Need to spruce up an old frame? Trim store! How about adding a trim to last year's skirt? . . . YES, head to the trim store. It's my answer to almost everything. This lace was not only a bargain, it's also a terrific way to jazz up some plain bangles.

## YOU'LL NEED

- Flat metal cuff about 2 inches wide (you'll probably want to make more than one!)
- 10 inches of lace trim (per cuff)*
- E-6000 glue
- Toothpicks
- ICE Resin
- Wax paper
- Disposable paintbrush
- Rubber or plastic gloves
- Small flat-back acrylic gems in colors that go with your lace
- * Your trim should be a little less than 2 inches wide or one that you can cut to size.

## HERE'S HOW

**1** With small dabs of E-6000 on a toothpick, neatly glue your lace on your cuff and let dry. You might need to cut it and overlap it for your design.

**2** If you need to, review the instructions on the ICE Resin and my tips on page 232. Mix about ⅛ cup of your resin outside using gloves. The fumes from resin can be harsh and you will need to work in a well-ventilated area.

**3** Place your cuff on wax paper and apply a very light coat of resin to the bangle, making sure to soak the lace. Let dry overnight in a room or area of the house that you don't use.

*Careful:*

Don't use too much resin because we don't want it to drip.

**4** Once the resin is dry, glue on the gems in different places until you're satisfied with how it looks.

# RESIN AND LACE EARRINGS

I've seen tons of earrings made from lace, but they always seem really flimsy to me. I decided to make them a little sturdier so they would last a lifetime and keep their shape forever.

## YOU'LL NEED

- Gold lace trim that would make great earrings
- ICE Resin
- Wax paper
- Disposable paintbrush
- Rubber or plastic gloves
- Drill with 1/16-inch drill bit
- 2 gold-tone earring wires
- 2 gold-tone jump rings
- Needle-nose pliers (and wirecutters if the pliers don't have them)

## HERE'S HOW

**1** Cut lace pieces in the shapes you want for your earrings.

**2** If you need to, review the instructions on the ICE Resin and my tips on page 232. Mix your resin outside using gloves. The fumes from resin can be harsh and you will need to work in a well-ventilated area. Put your lace pieces flat on some wax paper and then pour a small amount of resin on top of them so that they are coated but the resin is not running off the edges. Use a brush to smooth it out. Let dry overnight in a room or area of the house that you don't use.

**3** When the resin is dry, drill holes for the jump rings.

**4** Attach earring wires to the jump rings.

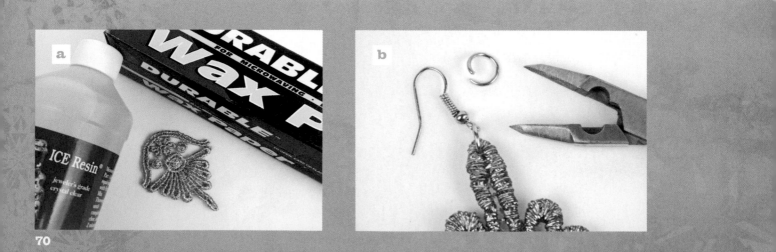

# GILDED LACE CUFF

So easy to make, and the best way to reuse an old bangle that might be tarnished! I think that this cuff would look great in almost any color. Use embroidered lace and watch it seem to transform into metal!

## YOU'LL NEED

- 1 piece of embroidered lace or lace trim about 6 inches long
- 3-inch flat metal cuff
- E-6000 glue
- Toothpicks
- ICE Resin
- Wax paper
- Disposable paintbrush
- Rubber or plastic gloves
- Krylon gray primer
- Krylon metallic gold

## HERE'S HOW

1  Using small dabs of E-6000 on a toothpick, glue your lace onto your cuff, just to keep it in place.

2  If you need to, review the instructions on the ICE Resin and my tips on page 232. Mix your resin outside using gloves. The fumes from resin can be harsh and you will need to work in a well-ventilated area. Place your cuff on wax paper and brush on the resin, making sure to coat it thoroughly so the lace soaks up all the resin. Let dry overnight in a room or area of the house that you don't use.

3  After the resin is set and your lace is hard as a rock, spray your cuff with the gray primer.

4  Spray your cuff with the metallic paint and let dry.

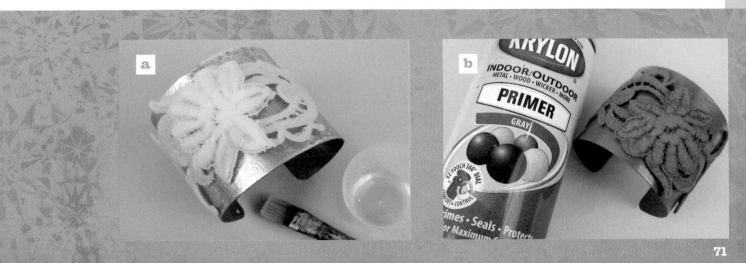

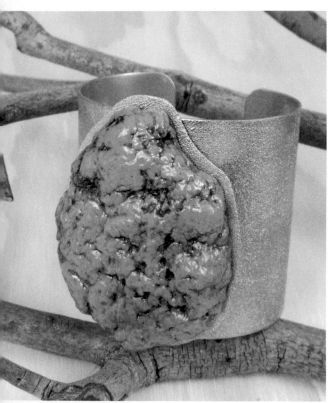

**W**hen you start writing a craft book and discover a brand-new technique, it's often hard to stop and move forward with other chapters because you're having way too much fun. That's what happened here. I made paper turquoise for weeks. I would start a batch, and then work on something else . . . and then immediately start another batch. I was *obsessed.* I hope you love this technique as much as I do. If you get your pieces just right, no one will know the difference, and they'll wonder how you found such a beautiful piece with such amazing stones.

# MAKING PAPER TURQUOISE

In a recent conversation with my mother, she told me that my younger brother Nate made a chunk of paper turquoise and put it on a macaroni necklace when he was in grade school, and it stopped people in their tracks when my mother wore it. So, apparently I'm old news. Still, this was just too fun not to share! By the way, this is the most fun I've ever had recycling. If you're impatient like me, I recommend drying these under a desk lamp.

## YOU'LL NEED

- Newspaper
- Scissors
- Blender
- Elmer's Glue-All
- Strainer with screen, (not holes) big enough to accommodate 1 batch
- Wax paper
- Acrylic paints in red, green, turquoise, blue, and black
- Paintbrushes
- Rags
- Minwax Polycrylic clear coat
- *Optional:* Desk lamp

## HERE'S HOW

1. Cut three large sheets of newspaper into strips about ½ inch wide.

2. Fill your blender about halfway with water and add shredded newspaper. Let it sit for about half an hour.

3. Blend the newspaper until you have mushy gray water.

4. Pour the mixture into the strainer and drain out about 90 percent of the water. At this point you can pick up the paper and squeeze out most of the rest of the water.

5. Gather up a ball of paper about the size of a baseball and add around ¼ cup of Elmer's glue. Knead it together.

6. Place wax paper on a plate or tray.

7. Form your mush into stone shapes or roll into spheres to create beads and stones, any and all sizes you want.

8. Put your stones or beads under a desk lamp to dry them quickly. Mine usually dry overnight. You can also let them air-dry, but this usually takes a day or two.

9. When they are completely dry, paint your stones or beads any colors (except black—that comes later) and let them dry. I like to mix blues and greens together to make the perfect turquoise colors.

10. Coat the stones with black paint, then quickly rub off the paint with a rag so that it's only in the cracks of the stones. If you need to dab on more color, you can.

11. Once your stones are dry and look the way you want them to look, apply several coats of Minwax Polycrylic to give them a glossy, beautiful finish.

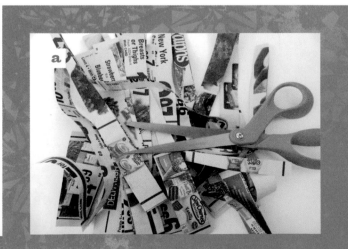

# PAPER TURQUOISE STITCHED LEATHER CUFF

Sometimes I feel big jewelry can be uncomfortable to wear because it's heavy. Not the case with this piece! With the paper turquoise and some leather, you can make big, chunky pieces and they're light as a feather. Now get out there and stop some traffic with this cuff!

## YOU'LL NEED

- Large paper turquoise stone (see directions and materials on page 74)
- Flat, thin cardboard
- Scissors
- Fiskars pinking shears
- Elmer's Glue-All
- ICE Resin
- Lumiere Sunset Gold metallic acrylic paint
- E-6000 glue
- Piece of leather (3 inches by 9 inches)
- Sewing machine with turquoise thread
- Snap set (or Velcro)
- Rubber or plastic gloves

## HeRE's HoW

1. Make a large paper turquoise stone for the center of the cuff.

2. Trace the stone on cardboard to determine the size of your setting and with regular scissors cut out three oval pieces in descending sizes (but all bigger than your turquoise stone). These will form your setting and make it look three-dimensional.

3. Go around the edges of the largest and smallest ovals with pinking shears to give some texture. Glue them together with Elmer's glue.

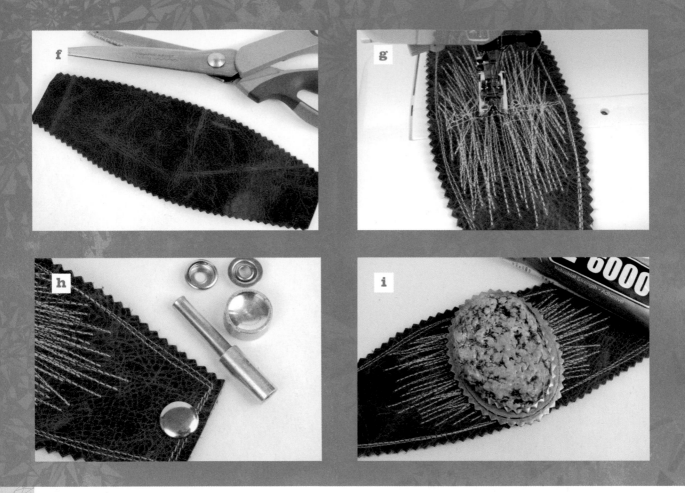

4  If you need to, review the instructions on the ICE Resin and my tips on page 232. Mix your resin outside using gloves. The fumes from resin can be harsh and you will need to work in a well-ventilated area. Brush the ovals with a small amount of resin and let set overnight in a room or area of the house that you don't use. This will make the cardboard as hard as a rock.

5  Paint the setting with the Lumiere metallic paint and let dry.

6  Glue your stone on the setting with E-6000 and let dry.

7  Cut your leather cuff in the shape you want using pinking shears. I chose a tapered shape as shown in photo f, using the pattern on page 365.

8  Stitch around the edges of your cuff and randomly in the center to create a design.

9  Measure your wrist and mark where you will place your snaps (or Velcro) and set in the snaps. Snap sets are easy to come by and very simple to use. Just follow the instructions they come with.

10  Glue the entire stone and setting on the center of the cuff with more E-6000 and let dry.

# TURQUOISE CONCH

This project is based on a conch belt I had when I was growing up, with a big silver buckle and a tiny piece of turquoise in the middle. As much as I loved it, I never found an occasion to wear it, but it was always one of my favorite possessions, and making this reminded me of it. Just thought I'd share that with you.

## You'll Need

- Flat, thin cardboard
- Scissors
- Elmer's Glue-All
- Fiskars pinking shears
- Three 1½-inch-diameter chunks of paper turquoise (see directions and materials on page 74)
- Wax paper
- ICE Resin
- Old paintbrush that you can throw away (for the resin)
- Lumiere metallic silver paint
- Small paintbrushes (for the paint and clear coats)
- Drill with small drill bit
- E-6000 glue
- 10 large silver-tone jump rings
- Needle-nose pliers (and wirecutters if the pliers don't have them)
- 2 pieces of silver-tone chain, each 4 inches long
- 1 lobster claw closure
- Minwax Polycrylic clear coat or Minwax Clear Brushing Lacquer
- Rubber or plastic gloves

## Here's How

1. Using the patterns on page 366, trace shapes on the cardboard and cut them out with regular scissors.

2. Glue them together with Elmer's glue.

3. Trace around your three chunks of paper turquoise on the cardboard shapes and cut out the shapes a bit larger than the line you traced using pinking shears. These will be your settings.

4. If you need to, review the instructions on the ICE Resin and my tips on page 232. Mix your resin outside using gloves. The fumes from resin can be harsh and you will need to work in a well-ventilated area.

5. Lay out all the pieces on wax paper and brush on the resin to coat them thoroughly. Let them dry on the wax paper overnight in a room or area of the house that you don't use.

6. Paint all the pieces with the Lumiere metallic silver paint and let them dry.

7. Drill holes on opposite sides of each piece.

8. Glue your turquoise chunks on the three corresponding pieces with E-6000.

9. Attach your pieces together with jump rings.

10. Add 4-inch piece of chain to each end.

11. Add jump rings and a lobster claw to the ends for closure.

# ZIGZAG TURQUOISE

This entire cuff is made from recycled materials, which couldn't make me happier. It's wonderful when something that might have gone into the garbage turns out this beautiful. I don't say this often, but in this case it's really true . . . THE POSSIBILITIES HERE ARE ENDLESS!

## YOU'LL NEED

- Cardboard (I like recycling the Medium Priority Shipping boxes from the post office)
- X-ACTO knife or boxcutter
- Elmer's Glue-All
- Clothespins
- Fiskars pinking shears
- Large chunk of paper turquoise (see directions and materials on page 74)
- Lumiere metallic paint in rust
- ICE Resin
- Old paintbrush that you can throw away
- Wax paper
- E-6000 glue
- Minwax Polycrylic clear coat or Minwax Clear Brushing Lacquer
- Rubber or plastic gloves

## HERE'S HOW

1. Cut a strip of cardboard 2½ inches by 9 inches and rub it over the edge of a counter to give it flexibility.

2. Roll the cardboard to create your cuff, making sure it's big enough to go over your hand comfortably. Use Elmer's glue to close the cuff and hold it in place with two clothespins while it dries.

3. Cut strips that measure 2½ inches by ⅜ inches with pinking shears and glue them around the cuff with more Elmer's glue and let dry. This is where you can create any kind of design you want.

4. Trace and then cut out with pinking shears a shape a bit larger than your piece of paper turquoise. This will be your setting.

5. If you need to, review the instructions on the ICE Resin and my tips on page 232. Mix your resin outside using gloves. The fumes from resin can be harsh and you will need to work in a well-ventilated area.

6. Place your cuff and setting on wax paper. Brush the pieces with resin, making sure the pieces are thoroughly coated but the resin is not drippy. Let dry overnight. This will make your cardboard pieces as strong as metal!

7  When the cardboard pieces are dry, paint them with the Lumiere metallic rust and let dry.

8  Glue the large piece of turquoise on the setting piece with E-6000. Now glue the finished stone and setting on the cuff with more E-6000.

9  Coat the entire cuff with Minwax Polycrylic or Minwax Clear Brushing Lacquer for a tough finish.

# SQUASH BLOSSOM

I love visiting my aunts in New Mexico and seeing all the wonderful ladies walking around in big turquoise jewelry. There are so many variations of turquoise, and mixed with either silver and gold, they're absolutely beautiful. I had a handful of faceted stone beads, but not enough to make a whole necklace, so I fashioned some paper turquoise beads and created this showstopper.

- Silver beading wire
- Needle-nose pliers
  (and wirecutters if the pliers don't have them)
- Silver-tone crimp beads
- 12 paper turquoise beads
  (see directions and materials
  on page 74)
- 14 large beads
- 1 large paper turquoise centerpiece stone
- 1 silver-tone lobster claw closure

## HeRE's How

1  Cut a piece of beading wire about 18 inches long.

2  Add a crimp bead then a lobster claw to the end.

3  Loop the end of the beading wire back through the crimp bead and crimp the bead with your needle-nose pliers.

4  String your beads, alternating large beads and paper turquoise beads. Remember to stop halfway and put your large turquoise chunk smack dab in the center.

5  To finish your necklace, add a crimp bead at each end, then loop the beading wire through a silver jump ring and back through the crimp bead. Pull the beading wire taut and crimp the bead with your needle-nose pliers.

6  Finish one side with a lobster claw for the closure and trim any excess beading wire.

# SEED BEAD–COVERED METAL CUFF

So, a while ago, I was watching *The Oprah Winfrey Show*, where I saw a woman who covered everything in her house with seed beads. I mean *everything*. Let's just say (without being judgy) that she seemed like kind of a nut. Then I got to thinking . . . this lady got herself booked with Oprah, and I've never even come close . . . so how much of a nut could she be? I covered these metal cuffs in seed beads and plan to contact Oprah's people as soon as this book hits shelves!

## YoU'LL NeED

- Turquoise stone or large bead (see directions and materials on page 74)
- Metal cuff bracelet (from the dollar store)
- Elmer's Glue-All
- Seed beads in matching or complementary color
- E-6000 glue
- Minwax Polycrylic clear coat

## HeRE's HoW

1. Glue your stone to the middle of the metal cuff with E-6000 and let dry.

2. Spread a thin layer of Elmer's glue on the rest of the cuff, sprinkle seed beads all over, and let dry.

3. Spread another coat of Elmer's glue on the bracelet and add another layer of seed beads, making sure to cover up any holes left on the bracelet.

4. Fill any holes or gaps around and underneath the stone with more glue and beads. so that it's like a setting of gems.

5. Keep adding layers of Elmer's glue and seed beads until it has the effect you want and the entire cuff is covered.

6. Finish with two or three coats of Minwax Polycrylic. Let dry for about ten to fifteen minutes between coats.

# REAL TURQUOISE AND BRASS STAMPED RINGS

I have been finding flat turquoise beads all over the place, so I decided to make a simple statement ring out of one. Check out www.amazon.com for a huge selection of turquoise beads that would work well for this project.

## YOU'LL NEED

- Real turquoise stones or flat paper turquoise stones, 1 inch by 1 inch or larger (see directions and materials on page 74)
- Stamped brass ornaments (see Resource Guide)
- E-6000 glue
- Dish towel
- Ring blanks

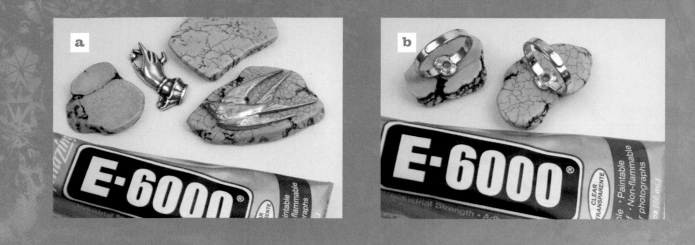

## HeRE's HoW

1. Glue your stamped brass ornament onto the turquoise and let dry.

2. Place your paper turquoise facedown on a crumpled dish towel, making sure the back presents a level surface for gluing.

3. With a generous amount of E-6000, glue the ring blank on, and let dry.

# TEXTURED METAL AND PAPER TURQUOISE CUFF

I have been trying for ages to figure out a way to give plain metal some texture. Other than hammering it, which looks amazing, I was stumped. Then one day the answer dawned on me. Embossing powder! Embossing powder is a fine powder that adds a raised texture to flat images when heated. It turned my crafty world upside-down.

## YOU'LL NEED

- Large chunk of paper turquoise (see directions and materials on page 74)
- Aluminum flashing
- Tin shears or heavy-duty scissors with serrated blades
- Scrap wood
- Flat metal cuff
- E-6000 glue
- Krylon gray primer
- Krylon Gold Metallic
- Elmer's Glue-All
- Gold embossing powder (www.createforless.com)
- Embossing heat gun or very hot hairdryer
- Minwax Clear Aerosol Lacquer

## HERE'S HOW

1. Cut a piece of aluminum flashing about 4 inches by 4 inches with tin shears or heavy-duty serrated scissors. Trace around your turquoise chunk on the flashing and cut out the shape, plus an extra ⅛ inch around the diameter.

2. Glue the shape to the metal cuff with the E-6000 and let dry.

3. Spray the entire cuff with gray primer and let dry.

4. Spray the cuff with metallic gold and let dry.

5. Coat your cuff with a thin coat of Elmer's glue. While it's still wet, sprinkle embossing powder to cover it. Shake or lightly blow off the excess.

6. Heat the cuff with your heat gun or a very hot blow dryer until the embossing powder bonds.

7. Spray the entire cuff in Minwax Clear Aerosol Lacquer to coat thoroughly

8. Glue on your paper turquoise stone with E-6000 and let dry.

# EASY-WEAR HARDWARE

Like many creative people I know, heading to the hardware store is part of my daily routine. I'm always looking for something interesting to use in my creations, and I rarely leave empty-handed. A while back I designed a room for the guy who owns my local hardware store, and we became good friends. Now, when something colorful and fun comes in, he calls me. The last call I got was about colorful mason twine and clear plastic tubing. He thought that I could use them in my next book. And he was right. Go, True Value in Silver Lake!

# A TINGE OF FRINGE

I love fringe. Even the word feels happy to me. When you think about it, things associated with fringe are always really fun. Like flappers in fringy flapper dresses; hula girls in their fringy grass skirts. And let's not forget Gypsy Rose Lee, the burlesque dancer who was never without something fringy to wow the crowds. For these cuffs, I made my own fringe from some colorful twine I picked up at the hardware store. Now, what could be more fun than wearing some fringe around your wrist? I say, not much!

## YOU'LL NEED

- Piece of vinyl
- Piece of cardboard
- Scissors
- E-6000 glue
- 8 yards of colorful mason twine
- Transparent tape
- Several pieces of ribbon, different widths, each 9 inches long
- Sewing machine
- 2-inch piece of sticky-back Velcro

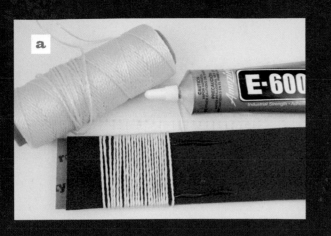

## HeRE's HoW

1 Cut a piece of vinyl 2 inches by 9 inches. Cut a piece of cardboard 2 inches by 10 inches and place the vinyl piece on top of the cardboard.

2 Squirt two small lines of E-6000 like railroad tracks along the edges of the vinyl.

3 Tape the end of the twine to the end of the cardboard and start wrapping the twine around the vinyl and cardboard, making sure each row of twine is right next to the other.

4 When you finish wrapping the twine, let the glue dry. Cut the fringe down the center of the back on the cardboard side. (As always, I find Fiskars to be the best scissors! Just sayin'.)

5 Stitch your ribbons on top of the vinyl to create stripes. Make sure to stitch along the ends of each side of the cuff to keep the fringe in place.

6 Trim your ends and fold over ½ inch. Stitch across the fold to create a clean edge as shown in photo e.

7 Stick the Velcro strips on the ends of your cuff for the closure.

*Hint:*
For added security, you can stitch the Velcro in place on the sewing machine.

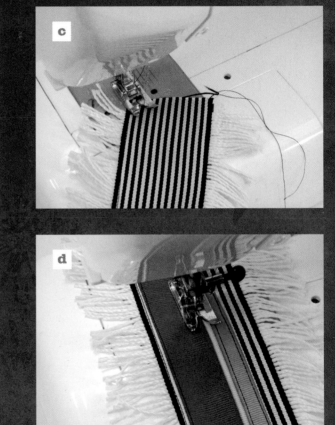

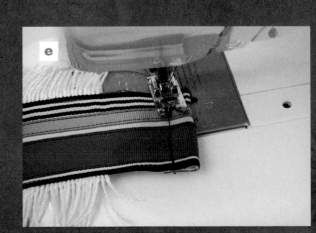

# GRAY PEARL AND CRYSTAL SHOE CLIPS

I found a roll of something called gutter guard at my local hardware store and have not been able to stop playing with it since. Something about the ease with which you can cut it and the perfectly spaced diamonds . . . it's really useful. Needless to say, I went nuts with it and I'm sure after this book is finally put to bed, I'll still be coming up with ideas for it. I hope you do, too. It's not very expensive at all and there is quite a bit of it in every roll, since gutters are usually the length of a house. (And how great is it that something called gutter guard can be transformed into glamorous shoe clips!)

## YOU'LL NEED

- Plastic gutter guard
- Scissors
- E-6000 glue
- Toothpicks
- 50 gray pearls
- 2 large ¾ inch x ¾ inch flat-back crystals (or experiment with what you have on hand)
- 2 clip-on earring blanks

## HERE'S HOW

**1** Cut a 4 inch by 8 inch piece of gutter guard into two triangle shapes measuring 7 x 7 x 6 grid squares, as shown in photo a, or in any shape you like.

**2** Using E-6000 on a toothpick, start adding pearls, making sure not to add any in the center area where your large crystal will be set.

**3** Set a crystal in the center of each triangle with a generous amount of E-6000 and let dry.

**4** Flip your piece over and glue the clip-on earring blanks toward the top of the clip, with the opening of the earring clips facing toward the toe. Make sure to glue on the wavy side, not the flat disk side, as shown in photo d.

# INNER TUBE TRIO

When I designed this trio, I thought of the beautiful summer jewelry that magazine stylists use in swimsuit photo shoots. I think these would look amazing worn when you're walking down the street on your summer vacation with a terrific cover-up against your sun-kissed skin. Well, that's how I picture it.

## YOU'LL NEED
## (FOR EACH NECKLACE)

- ¼ yard of solid knit fabric
- Scissors
- 3 to 4 inches of ½-inch-diameter clear plastic tubing
- 14 inches of medium chain
- E-6000 glue
- Hot glue gun and glue sticks

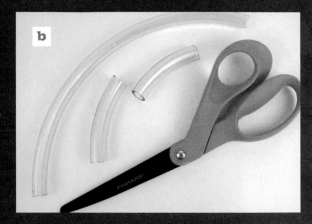

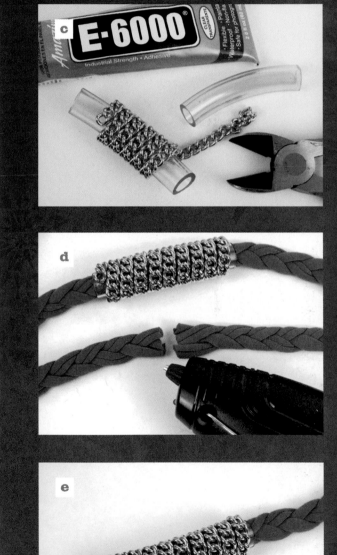

## HeRE's HoW

1. Cut three 1-inch strips along the entire width of your fabric—that is, side to side, not lengthwise. (Most fabrics are 45 inches or 60 inches wide.)

2. Carefully braid the strips from top to bottom.

3. Cut the plastic tubing in 3-inch and 4-inch lengths.

4. Glue the chain around the plastic tubing with dabs of E-6000 glue, making sure to be neat and tidy, and let dry.

5. Slip the chain-wrapped tubing over the knit braid.

6. Glue together the ends of the braid with hot glue. I really like the way hot glue works with fabric. It makes a terrific bond.

7. Slip the tube over the hot-glued ends.

### Hint:
If the tube slips, add a dab of hot glue inside the end of the tube to keep it in place.

# LAUNDRY BAG

If you're wondering why I call this the Laundry Bag, I'll tell you. The decorative rope is laundry line and I got it at the dollar store. You can find it all over the place in different colors, and I thought it was just too good to pass up. The best part about it is that it's nylon and it won't lose its color. When I was growing up, my parents brought back a yarn tapestry from Mexico and the technique I used here is reminiscent of that very tapestry. (I wonder what happened to it?)

## You'll Need

- 1 sturdy handbag in need of a makeover
- Scissors
- 3 different colors of laundry rope (you could also use twine or heavy yarn)
- Hot glue gun and glue sticks
- 40 medium and large flat-back acrylic gems
- E-6000 glue
- 2 clothespins

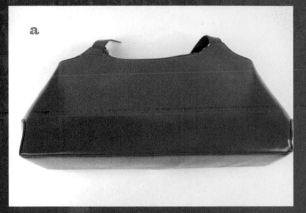

a

## Here's How

1. Cut the handles off the bag, leaving about 3 inches of each handle. You will need those pieces later to fold over and create a loop for your new handles.

2. Figure out a swirly design that you like. Or you could just go for it, like I did, and see what happens. Either way, it will look terrific.

3. Using your hot glue gun, start with a dot of glue in the center and work your way outward, gluing the laundry line into a spiral. Be careful with the glue, making sure to get it only under your swirls.

4. Figure out how big you want your adjoining swirl to be and start to glue that down with the hot glue, this time working your way to the center of the swirl.

5. Cut the end and tuck it into the center of the swirl.

6. Cover the centers of your swirls with gems.

7. Continue making swirls until the entire bag is covered, front and back.

8. For the handle, cut a piece of laundry line 18 inches long.

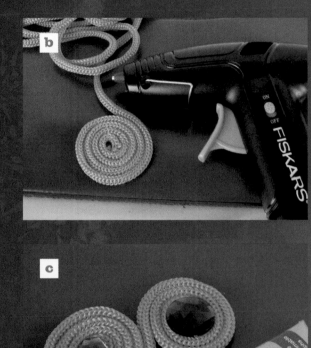

b

c

d

**9** Fold the ends in evenly to create a 9-inch handle and glue the ends together as shown in photo e.

**10** Take a long piece of laundry line and glue it to the end of the handle, leaving a 1-inch loop hanging out.

**11** Hot-glue the rope around and around the folded piece of laundry line until you get to the end. Leave a 3-inch piece hanging. You will tuck that through the handbag loops later and secure it with E-6000.

**12** Put the cut-off ends of your handbag straps through the loops on the ends of the new handles. Add a gob of E-6000, clamp with clothespins, and let dry.

**13** Tuck the extra piece of laundry line inside the folded-over part of your handbag strap and secure with more E-6000.

*Suggestion:*
You can also use twine, yarn, or any type of rope for this project. Heck, try using all three!

# ROPES AND CHAINS

These are two of the very first projects I made for this book, and I immediately fell in love with them. Something about using unexpected materials to create something beautiful just turns me on. There are all kinds of variations possible for this design, and I hope that if you make a different version, you'll share it with me. I also hope you'll love this project as much as I do.

## YoU'LL NeED

### FOR THE RED AND BLUE CUFF

- Aluminum flashing
- Tin shears or heavy-duty scissors with serrated blades
- Scrap wood
- Hot glue gun and glue sticks
- E-6000 glue
- 2 feet of red laundry line, thick twine, or rope
- 6 inches of blue laundry line, thick twine, or rope
- 2 feet of silver-tone ball chain
- Toothpicks
- 2-inch-wide flat, silver-tone metal cuff
- Large silver-tone beads

### FOR THE ORANGE AND GOLD CUFF

- 2-inch-wide flat, gold-tone metal cuff
- 2 feet of orange laundry line, rope, or thick twine
- 2 feet of gold-tone ball chain

## HeRE's HoW

### FOR THE RED AND BLUE CUFF

1. With tin shears or heavy-duty serrated scissors, cut a piece of aluminum flashing 3 inches by 3 inches. Draw a 2½-inch-diameter circle on the piece of flashing and cut that out.

2. Alternating dabs of hot glue and E-6000, glue down an end of the blue laundry line in the center of the circle and wrap it in a spiral shape until you've created a circle with a 1-inch diameter.

3. Glue red laundry line around the blue, leaving about ¼ inch of flashing around the edge of the circle.

4. With dabs of E-6000 on a toothpick, spread glue around the edge and carefully wrap your ball chain around the circle until you've reached the end of the flashing.

5. On each side of the cuff, glue and wrap the red laundry line in circles with the tail of the laundry line trailing toward the center of the cuff, but not all the way. You will need a flat surface in the center to glue your circle.

6. With dabs of E-6000 on a toothpick, spread glue around the edge of the red circles and surround them with more silver ball chain.

7. Glue your circle on top with E-6000 and let dry.

8. Glue silver balls in the center of the red side circles and the blue and red circle and let dry.

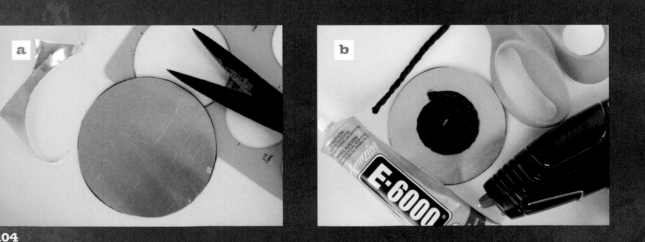

## FOR THE ORANGE AND GOLD CUFF

1. Carefully glue three spiral circles onto your cuff using the orange rope. Make sure to tuck the ends under the wrapping so it looks neat. Use alternate dabs of hot glue and E-6000 to keep the rope in place.

2. Spread E-6000 around the edges of your orange circles with a toothpick, surround them with the gold tone ball chain twice, and let dry.

# LITE-BRITES

Wow, I remember my Lite-Brite from when I was growing up. Okay, actually, I still have it and play with it from time to time, so you could argue that I haven't officially grown up YET. Oh well. I digress . . . There is something rewarding about putting bright little objects in specific holes to create cool patterns. Though the colors in this bangle are random, I still got the same thrill I get when I play with my Lite-Brite. I think you will, too.

## YOU'LL NEED

- Plastic gutter guard
- Scissors
- E-6000 glue
- Toothpicks
- Plastic pony beads (createforless.com has an amazing selection, from iridescent to fluorescent)
- 2 large clothespins

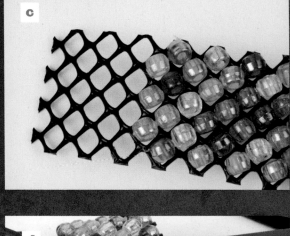

# HeRE's HoW

**1** Measure and cut a piece of gutter guard 2½ inches wide and as long as the circumference of your bangle, plus 1½ inches. For example, if your bangles will be 8 inches around, cut the gutter guard 9½ inches long.

**2** Starting on one end of your gutter guard, use E-6000 on a toothpick, spread some glue in a row of holes, and fill with pony beads.

**3** Continue until you have filled the grid, but make sure to leave 1½ inches on one end of your gutter guard without beads. This will be your overlap and part of the bangle closure.

**4** When the beads are in place and dry, add more E-6000 to the end of the gutter guard without beads and use clothespins to clamp the ends together until they dry. One end will fit into the other like a puzzle.

*Note:*
This bracelet is flexible because E-6000 is flexible.

# TUBULAR SENSATION

This is perhaps the most glamorous of all my hardware creations, and I hope it sparks your creativity in many different ways. Plastic tubing is usually sold by the foot, and it can be made into all kinds of different things. I happen to like wrapping it, but you could even paint it and cut it into smaller beads. Just enjoy the sensation!

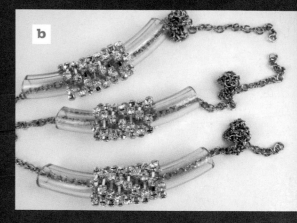

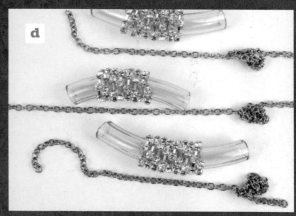

## ✦ YOU'LL NEED

- 13 inches of ½-inch clear plastic tubing
- Scissors
- E-6000 glue
- 1½ yards of crystal chain
- 70 inches of medium silver-tone chain
- Needle-nose pliers (and wirecutters if the pliers don't have them)
- Lobster claw closure
- 3 silver-tone jump rings

## HERE'S HOW

**1** Cut your plastic tubing into three 3-inch sections and two 2-inch sections.

**2** Dab E-6000 around the tubes. Wrap each of your 3-inch tubes with 1 foot of crystal chain, and wrap the 2-inch tubes with 10 inches of crystal chain. You can use less or more, depending on your style. Let dry.

**3** Create a choker about 16 inches long by adding jump rings and a lobster claw at the ends for the closure.

**4** String the two 2-inch crystal tubes onto the chain.

**5** Between the 2-inch crystal tubes, add a jump ring with three pieces of 18-inch chain attached to it.

**6** Add a 3-inch tube to each of the chains. Tie the ends of each chain in a knot. Keep knotting until the tube cannot slip over the knot and is held in place. Do this at three different levels.

109

# TU-BE OR NOT TU-BE

This has a distinct rock 'n' roll feel. Maybe even a little punk rock, don't you think? I particularly like the weight of this project, and the fact that you can use either silver- or gold-tone chain. Because the plastic tubing is transparent, these chokers will match ANY outfit or piercing!

## YOU'LL NEED

### FOR THE SHORTER CHOKER

- 34 inches of medium silver- or gold-tone chain
- Needle-nose pliers (and wirecutters if the pliers don't have them)
- 2 jump rings, silver or gold to match chain
- 1 lobster claw closure, silver or gold to match chain
- 4 inches of ½-inch-diameter clear plastic tubing
- Scissors
- E-6000 glue

### FOR THE LONGER CHOKER

- 32 inches of medium silver- or gold-tone chain
- Needle-nose pliers (and wirecutters if the pliers don't have them)
- 2 jump rings, silver or gold to match chain
- 1 lobster claw closure, silver or gold to match chain
- 8 inches of ½-inch-diameter plastic tubing
- Scissors
- E-6000 glue
- 28 inches of a different medium chain to wrap the ½-inch tubes

## HERE's HOW

### FOR THE SHORTER CHOKER

1. Cut a 16-inch piece of chain and add a jump ring on both ends and the lobster claw on one side to create your choker.

2. Dab E-6000 along the 4-inch tube, wrap the chain around it, and let dry.

3. Slip the chain through the tube, and you're ready to go.

### FOR THE LONGER CHOKER

1. Cut two 16-inch pieces of chain and add a jump ring on the ends plus the lobster claw on one side to create a double-strand choker.

2. Cut three 2-inch pieces of tubing and four ½-inch pieces.

3. Cut 3 pieces, 9 inches each from your second type of chain. Dab E-6000 along the two ½-inch tubes, wrap 9 inches of the second chain around each, and let dry.

4. Slip your tubes onto your chain and it's ready to wear.

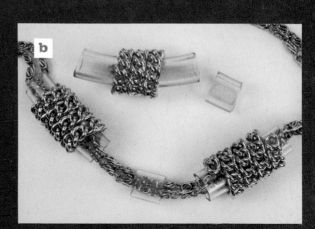

# PEARL AND DIAMOND CHOKER AND EARRINGS

While making this set I was brought back to the '80s for some reason. Maybe it was the geometric shapes? Maybe it was because I thought these would look supercool on a Patrick Nagel model? I don't know. Some people are carried back to a certain moment in time by a scent. I shoot back in time when I'm creating something. Weird, I know.

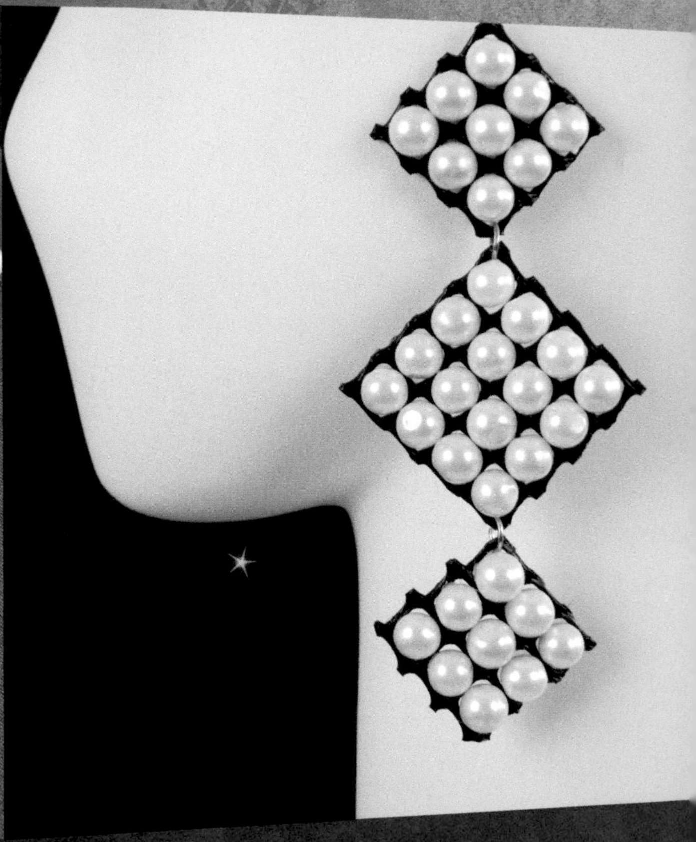

## YOU'LL NEED

### FOR THE CHOKER

- Plastic gutter guard
- Scissors
- E-6000 glue
- Toothpicks
- 11 gold-tone jump rings
- 2 pieces of black chain, each 6 inches long
- Needle-nose pliers (and wirecutters if the pliers don't have them)
- 1 large gold-tone lobster claw closure
- 93 pearls

### FOR THE EARRINGS

- Plastic gutter guard
- E-6000 glue
- Toothpicks
- 68 pearls
- 2 clip-on earring blanks

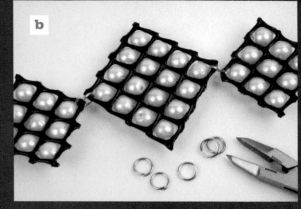

# HeRE's HoW

## FOR THE CHOKER

**1** Cut three 4 by 4 squares and five 3 by 3 squares from the gutter guard

**2** With dabs of E-6000 on a toothpick, starting at one end of a gutter guard piece, spread some glue in a row of holes, and fill each hole with a pearl. Continue until you have filled up the holes, and let dry.

**3** Add jump rings in between the squares to create your choker.

**4** Cut two 6-inch pieces of chain and attach a chain to the choker on each side with jump rings, and finish the ends with jump rings and a lobster claw for the closure.

## FOR THE EARRINGS

**1** Cut two 4 by 4 squares of gutter guard. Cut four 3 by 3 squares.

**2** Using E-6000 on a toothpick, carefully glue a pearl into each gutter guard space and let dry.

**3** Add jump rings between the squares and join at the corners to create dangle earrings.

**4** Using a generous amount of E-6000, add clip-on earring blanks to the top squares and let dry.

# TWINE AND TWINE AGAIN

Strolling down the aisle of my local hardware store, I found amazing twines and ropes in very beautiful colors. Though this project could be completed with lots of different materials, from yarns to thin pieces of fabric, something about the sheen and intensity of the colors of the mason twine got my attention. A few minutes later I ran into some no. 6 plastic chain in a different aisle, and soon this project was born. Can't you just see this piece walking down the runway with a neon one-piece bathing suit and a huge hat? I sure can.

## ✦ YOU'LL NEED
## FOR THE NECKLACE

- Mason twine in three different colors
- 1½ yards white plastic chain (no. 6 or smaller)
- Dritz Fray Check
- Scissors
- Needle-nose pliers (and wirecutters if the pliers don't have them)

## YOU'LL NEED
## FOR THE BRACELET ✦

- Mason twine in three different colors
- 27 inches of white plastic chain (no. 6 or smaller)
- Dritz Fray Check
- 8 large silver-tone jump rings
- 1 silver-tone lobster claw closure
- Scissors
- Needle-nose pliers (and wirecutters if the pliers don't have them

## HERE'S HOW
## FOR THE NECKLACE

1. Cut three pieces of chain, 16 inches, 17 inches, and 18 inches long.

2. Cut about 30 pieces of twine 6 inches long in each color (90 pieces altogether).

3. Using one color per length of chain, tie the 6-inch pieces on each link from one end to the other.

4. Secure each knot with a drop of Dritz Fray Check and let dry. This will keep it in place without discoloring the twine.

5. Add more ties if you feel your masterpiece isn't full enough.

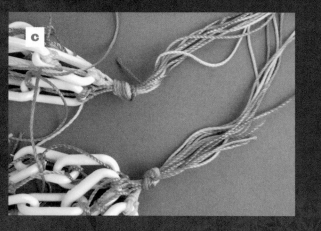

**6** Cut two 14-inch strands of twine in each color and knot the corresponding colors at the end of the length of chain. Finish ends with Dritz Fray Check.

**7** Repeat step 6 on the other side.

**8** Knot all the strands together as shown in photo c and secure with more Fray Check.

**9** Tie the knotted strands in a bow at the back for a closure.

## FOR THE BRACELET

**1** Cut two pieces of chain: 7 inches and 8 inches long.

**2** Cut about 20 pieces of twine 6 inches long in each color (at least 60 pieces altogether).

**3** Using one color on one length of chain and two colors on another, tie the 6-inch pieces on each link from one end to the other.

**4** Secure each knot with a drop of the Fray Check and let dry. This will keep it in place without discoloring the twine.

**5** Add more ties if you feel your masterpiece isn't full enough.

**6** Place a jump ring at each end of the three lengths of chain.

**7** Attach the jump rings together with one more jump ring on one end and a jump ring and lobster claw on the other end.

# TWINE NOT? EARRINGS

I've noticed lately that anything goes these days when it comes to personal style, and I couldn't be happier. Why do we have to follow rules when it comes to dress? As long as you're happy with how you look, that's all that matters! These superfunky earrings are made with ordinary items I found at the hardware store. I'm sure you can come up with versions that will reflect exactly who you are.

## YOU'LL NEED

- Mason twine in three different colors
- 4 links of white plastic chain (no. 6)
- 2 large silver-tone jump rings
- 2 silver-tone earring wires
- Dritz Fray Check
- Scissors
- Needle-nose pliers (and wirecutters if the pliers don't have them)

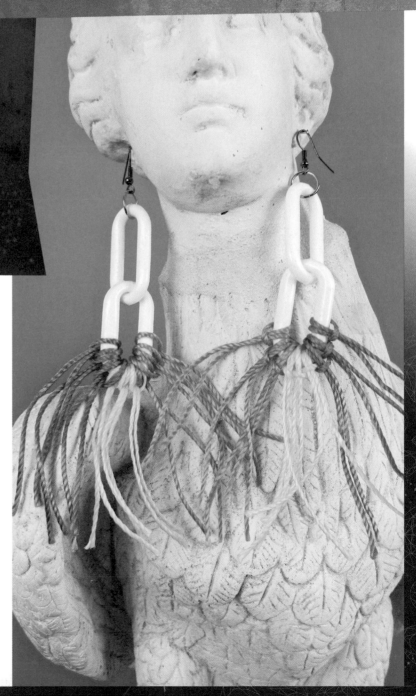

## HeRE's HoW

1. Cut about six pieces of twine 8 inches long in each color (18 pieces altogether).

2. Take three pieces of each color and tie them around one link of each earring. Secure each knot with a drop of the Dritz Fray Check and let dry. This will keep it in place without discoloring the twine.

3. Cut the chain into two pieces of two links each. Put a jump ring and an earring wire on the top link of each earring.

# TASTE THE RAINBOW

This one is for the kids at camp! Use whatever you have at hand, and have fun with it. Isn't that what crafting is all about anyway? Learn the rules and then break them! Have fun and don't call me until the end of summer when I have to pick you up. Love, DAD

## YOU'LL NEED

- Plastic gutter guard
- Scissors
- Yarn in several different colors
- Strips of fabric in any color
- Vinyl or leather scraps in several different colors
- 1 large flat-back gem
- Fiskars pinking shears
- E-6000 glue
- 1 ponytail band
- 1 large button
- Needle and thread

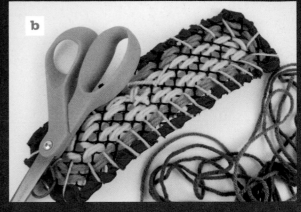

## HeRE's HoW

1. Cut a piece of gutter guard 3 inches by 8 inches. Weave your fabric strips around the edges. This will soften the edges and give the piece a nice frame. Don't worry if you have to tie knots; it will give it more texture.

2. Weave your yarns in a spiral, working from the outside edges in toward the center, changing colors as you like.

3. Tie off the yarn with a knot.

4. Using pinking shears, cut your vinyl scraps into circles of various sizes ranging from ¾ inch to 3 inches in diameter.

5. Stack them in sets of four or five, starting with the largest on the bottom, glue them together with the E-6000, and let dry.

6. Glue the gem on the center of your vinyl centerpiece and let dry.

7. Loop a ponytail band around the end of your cuff as shown in photo d.

8. Sew a button on the other end of your cuff. This is what the ponytail band will loop around to make the closure.

9. Glue the vinyl circle onto your cuff in the center with E-6000 and let dry.

'm always a bit confused about when to call something a "mixed-media" piece. Since I spend the majority of my days gluing random things to other random things, I would say that almost everything I do is mixed media in one way or another. Long ago I changed my motto from JUST DO IT to JUST GLUE IT! These pieces definitely have a distinct mixed-media flair and I'm sure with your creativity you will be able to make something even more amazing. I can't wait to see what you make!

# MONA LISA MIXED-MEDIA BROOCH

Do you ever just look in your craft box and wonder what to do with all the bits and pieces of projects from days gone by? Well here's the answer! This mixed-media brooch can be made any number of ways with whatever you have left lying around. Change the image, use an old photograph, or make a collage. It's up to you!

## YOU'LL NEED

- Flat, thin cardboard
- Book pages
- Elmer's Glue-All
- Small image of the *Mona Lisa* (my artwork for this project is on page 377)
- 1-inch flat paintbrush
- Minwax Polycrylic clear coat
- Scissors
- Toothpicks
- Fabric
- 10 inches of ¾-inch ribbon
- Fabric flowers
- Crystal chain
- Large flat-back acrylic gems
- Small piece of jewelry or part of an old earring
- Pearls
- 3 inches of long fringe
- E-6000 glue
- Hot glue gun and glue sticks
- Pin back
- Needle-nose pliers (and wirecutters if the pliers don't have them)
- 5-inch piece of 20-gauge wire
- *Optional:* Sewing machine if you want to stitch the ribbon like I did

## Here's How

1. Cut your cardboard in an oval about 4 inches by 3 inches.

2. Cut out an oval from your book page a bit bigger than the cardboard oval. Fringe the edges, and with your paintbrush and some watered-down Elmer's, glue the book page to the cardboard, folding the fringed edges around the back of the cardboard.

3. Trace the oval again on a book page, cut out the shape, and glue it onto the oval so that it covers the back.

4. Cut out your image, and with more Elmer's glue, adhere it to the oval.

5. Coat the entire front and back in Minwax Polycrylic and let dry.

6. With dabs of E-6000 on a toothpick, carefully add your flowers, crystals, pearls, and jewelry pieces to the outer edge of your oval.

7. Cut 3 inches of wire and make a loop as shown in photo b.

8. Cut a strip from the fabric 10 inches long and 1½ inches wide. On the sewing machine, stitch your ribbon on top of the fabric strip to give it some interest.

9. Tie it in a bow and glue it just under Mona's neck.

10. Bend 2 inches of the wire in half to make a loop and hot-glue it to the end of the ribbon. While hot-gluing, wrap the ribbon around the wire to make your tassel.

11. Slip your wire tassel loop onto the wire loop, glue it to the bottom of the oval, and let dry.

12. Glue on your pin back with E-6000 and you're done!

# MIXED-MEDIA NECKLACE

I'm sure that you will take this project and run with it, because I already know how supercreative you are. What I love about this project is that I could use everyday items from around the house for it. I know if you dig in your craft box, you'll be able to create this necklace, and something even more spectacular. Make sure you send me a photo when you're done, okay?

## ★ You'll Need

- Flat, thin cardboard
- Elmer's Glue-All
- Image you like that will fit on the oval (my artwork for this project is on page 375)
- 1-inch flat paintbrush
- Book pages
- Minwax Polycrylic clear coat
- Scissors
- Toothpicks
- Ribbon
- Fabric flower
- Crystal chain
- Small piece of jewelry or part of an old earring
- Scraps of lace
- E-6000 glue
- 18 inches of black chain
- Lobster claw closure
- 3 jump rings
- Needle-nose pliers (and wirecutters if the pliers don't have them)
- 3 inches of 20-gauge wire
- *Optional:* Sewing machine if you want to stitch the ribbon like I did

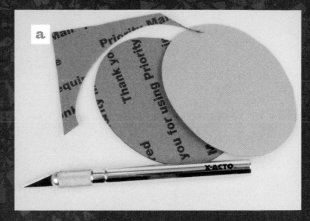

## Here's How

**1** Cut your cardboard in an oval about 4 inches by 3 inches.

**2** Cut out an oval from your book page a bit bigger than your cardboard oval. Fringe the edges, and with your paintbrush and some watered-down Elmer's, glue the book page to the cardboard, folding the fringed edges around the back of the cardboard oval.

**3** Trace the oval again on a book page, cut it out, and glue it onto the oval so that it covers the back.

4. Cut out your image and with more Elmer's, glue it to the oval.

5. Coat the entire front and back in the Minwax Polycrylic and let dry.

6. With dabs of E-6000 on a toothpick carefully add your chain to the outer edges of the oval.

7. Add your lace and jewelry pieces, and finally add your ribbon flower.

8. Cut a 3-inch piece of wire and make a loop as shown in photo e. Glue it to the back of the oval with E-6000 so that it sticks out over the top edge by about ½ inch. This is where you will hang your chain and tie your ribbon.

9. On the sewing machine, stitch your ribbon to give it some texture. For a really nice touch, you could add some hand stitching instead.

10. Tie it in a bow around the wire loop.

11. Attach a jump ring to the exact center of your chain and loop the cameo onto it.

12. Add jump rings on the ends of the chains and a lobster claw for the closure.

# SEEING HEART

I was with my friend Erica at an art gallery this year, wandering through rows and rows of paintings, when I saw a portrait of a medieval man with a heart painted on his chest and an eye painted on the heart. It completely inspired this piece of jewelry and reminds me of a wonderful day spent with a friend enjoying art. I know it seems like this project requires a lot of supplies, but you can alter it depending on what you have around the house.

## YOU'LL NEED

- 22 inches of 1-inch satin ribbon
- Plastic gutter guard
- 18 pearls
- E-6000 glue
- Toothpicks
- Hammer and nail
- Scrap wood
- Aluminum flashing
- Medal or charm
- Images of eye and heart (my artwork is on pages 375–76)
- Flat, thin cardboard
- Elmer's Glue-All
- Scissors
- 2 large jump rings
- Red acrylic paint
- Lumiere metallic bronze paint
- Tin shears or heavy-duty scissors with serrated blades
- Paintbrushes (for the paint)
- ICE Resin
- Disposable paintbrush
- Krylon black Fusion for Plastic
- Rubber or plastic gloves

## HERE'S HOW

1. Copy the eye and heart patterns on pages 375–76 on plain white paper (or copy the heart on red paper and save a step).

2. Glue the heart to the cardboard with Elmer's glue and then cut it out.

3. With tin shears or heavy-duty serrated scissors, cut a piece from the aluminum flashing 4 inches by 6 inches. Trace the heart shape with an additional ¼-inch border all the way around onto the flashing. Cut out the heart shape from the flashing.

4. Put the heart on a piece of scrap wood so that you don't ruin your work surface. Tap a hole in the top and bottom of the heart with your hammer and nail.

5. Paint the heart red and let dry and then paint gold rays from the center.

6. Glue the eye on the heart with Elmer's glue.

7. If you need to, review the instructions on the ICE Resin and my tips on page 232. Mix your resin outside using gloves. The fumes from resin can be harsh and you will need to work in a well-ventilated area. Coat the entire piece of cardboard in resin and let dry overnight in a room or area of the house that you don't use. This will make it jewelry quality and give it a wonderful finish.

8. Spray-paint the tin heart black.

9. Cut your gutter guard in a diamond or square 1 inch by 1 inch with two extra diamonds on opposite corners.

10. With dabs of E-6000 on a toothpick, fill the center grid with pearls. Be neat! Repeat for the second piece.

11. Glue your cardboard heart on the tin heart with E-6000.

12. Hang your medal or charm from the bottom of the heart on a jump ring.

13. Cut a second piece of gutter guard in a diamond or square 1 inch by 1 inch with two small diamonds at each end as in photo g. With dabs of E-6000 on a toothpick, glue in your pearls.

14. Thread ribbon through the extra diamond spaces on the corners of the pearled gutter guard pieces so that they slide into place.

15. Hang your heart centerpiece between the pearl sliders with another jump ring.

16. Close the choker by tying it behind your neck with the extra ribbon.

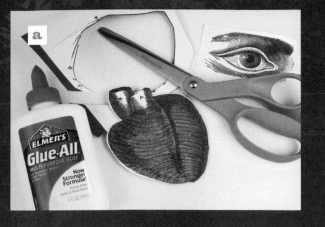

a

b

c

d

e

f

g

h

# LOVE HANDCUFFS

Ah, romance! Nothing like it! When you're falling in love, the entire world just seems wonderful. I used a love letter for this project, but you can use a favorite poem, short story, inspirational quotes or whatever you want. As for me, I love the idea of having a love letter around your wrist. It seems, well, poetic.

## YOU'LL NEED

- 1-inch bangle
- Elmer's Glue-All
- ½-inch flat paintbrush
- Copy of love letter
- Minwax Polycrylic clear coat
- Lumiere metallic paint in gold

## HeRE's HoW

**1** Cut your love letter in strips, keeping them in the order in which they should be read.

**2** Using a brush and watered-down Elmer's glue, glue the strips around and around your cuff making sure to only slightly overlap each strip so that the bangle doesn't show through.

**3** Continue until you've covered the entire bangle.

**4** When your bangle is covered, coat it with several coats of Minwax Polycrylic to seal and protect it. Let each coat dry for about 15 minutes before applying the next one.

### Hint:
I used a very small bit of Lumiere metallic gold paint over one bangle to give it some shimmer. Give it a try!

# LOVE IN A BOTTLE

I put this love letter on my copy machine and made it as tiny as possible. Then it sat on my desk for a month before I decided what to do with it. It wasn't until Valentine's Day was just around the corner that inspiration hit . . . and this was the result. You really could put anything in this little glass vial, but I chose a love letter. It seemed so romantic. Adding charms is your choice. I used hearts and keys, but it's up to you.

## YOU'LL NEED

- Small glass vial with cork top (make sure the vial has a lip around the mouth)
- 20 inches of delicate silver-tone chain
- Several silver-tone hearts
- Silver-tone key charm
- 5 silver-tone jump rings
- 1 silver-tone lobster claw closure
- Love letter (and access to a copy machine that reduces images)
- Needle-nose pliers (and wirecutters if the pliers don't have them)

## HeRE's How

1. Cut 20 inches of chain, then cut 2 inches off that.

2. Wrap the 18-inch piece of chain around the neck of the glass vial at the 9-inch mark and secure with a jump ring so that it's snug around the lip.

3. With another jump ring add the 2-inch piece of chain to the longer chain so that the 2-inch piece hangs free.

4. Add a heart to the end of the smaller chain.

5. Add a key to the smaller chain, or at the neck, wherever you think it looks best.

6. Shrink your love letter on a copy machine so that it will fit into the vial (about 1½ inches by 1½ inches).

7. Roll it into a tube, slip it inside the vial, and close with the cork. You could tie it with a small ribbon or piece of thread.

8. Add jump rings and a lobster claw to the ends of the chain and go show off your love.

### Other Ideas For This Project:
Birthday wishes, small photos, best friend pendants.

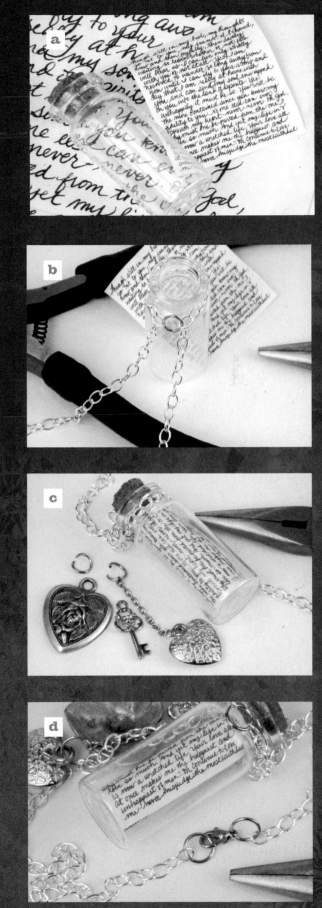

# WEARING MY WISHES

I believe in good-luck charms and putting things out into the universe. This necklace is the perfect way to do both and look chic at the same time. Replace the wishes or carry one for a friend and fill your glass bottle (and your life) with all the magic that you can.

## YOU'LL NEED

- Small glass vial with cork top (make sure the vial has a lip around the mouth)
- 20 inches of delicate gold chain (or make this any length you want)
- Several gold-tone charms
- Gold-tone key charm
- 5 gold-tone jump rings
- 1 gold-tone lobster claw closure
- List of wishes and access to a copy machine that reduces images
- Needle-nose pliers (and wirecutters if the pliers don't have them)

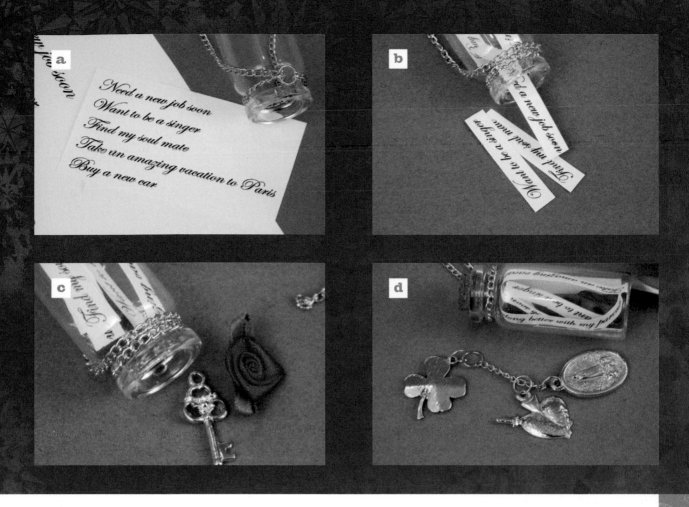

## HeRE's HoW

1. Cut 20 inches of chain, then cut 2 inches off that.

2. Wrap your 18-inch piece of chain around the neck of the glass vial at the 9-inch mark and secure with a jump ring so that it's snug around the lip.

3. With another jump ring add the 2-inch piece of chain to the longer chain so that the 2-inch piece hangs free.

4. Add a charm to the end of the smaller chain.

5. Add more charms to the smaller chain or at the neck, wherever you think they look best.

6. Shrink your list of wishes on a copy machine so that it will fit into the vial—about 1½ inches by 1½ inches. Cut the wishes into separate strips so they can be read easily.

7. Slip them inside the vial and close with the cork.

8. Add jump rings and a lobster claw to the ends of the chain for the closure.

9. Take out your wishes when they come true and replace them with new ones!

### Other Ideas For This Project:
Birthday wishes, small photos, best friend pendants!

I honestly don't think I've ever had more fun with any craft project than I've had with my Fuseworks microwave glass kiln. Melting glass in my kitchen has been a true adventure, and it allowed me to make pieces for this book that I never would have been able to make otherwise. Rarely do I go nuts over a particular product, but this glass kiln has changed the way I create. YOU WILL LOVE IT! Go to www.diamondtechcrafts.com and tell them Mark Montano sent you! Now, if you can't wait for your kiln to arrive to make some of the projects in this chapter, I would suggest using large beads or paper turquoise (see page 74 for instructions and materials).

# GLASS FUSING

I was the kid who always put a glass bottle in the campfire at the end of the night just to see if it would melt flat by morning. I LOVE MELTING GLASS. Two years ago I was sent the Fuseworks Microwave Kiln Kit, and it hasn't left my kitchen counter since! Everyone who visits me insists on making something with it because it's just so fun to use and experiment with. I'm not kidding. I promise that once you get started with this kiln, you will zip through the projects in this chapter and go on to make hundreds more.

# THINGS YOU NEED TO KNOW
## *(and Things I Learned After Two Years of Fusing)*

The glass fused in this kiln (and the inside of the kiln itself) can reach 1,400 to 1,600 degrees Fahrenheit. It's not a toy! It is not for children under the age of 16 without adult supervision.

DO NOT leave the microwave unattended while using this kiln and never heat longer than six minutes. In fact, I've found four minutes is the longest I've ever needed for any piece of glass.

There must be a minimum of 3 inches between the top of the kiln and the ceiling of your microwave.

Make sure that you leave room around your glass pieces when you place them in the kiln so that when you fuse, the glass doesn't melt and touch the side of the kiln, as this can ruin your kiln. I did get a bit of glass on the side of my kiln and was able to gently chip it off (when the kiln had completely cooled) and it still worked well, but it's better to be safe!

IMPORTANT! Let your pieces cool at least 20 minutes with the kiln lid on. You don't want your glass to cool too quickly—it may develop cracks or shatter. You want the glass to cool slowly and evenly so that it is extremely strong. This is called *annealing*.

Wear safety glasses AND cotton gloves when

handling the kiln and glass. Treat every piece of glass like *hot* glass because it can look cool but still be very HOT!

Keep a journal of your experiments with your glass pieces, logging details like how long you fused certain glass pieces and the types of glass you use.

NOTE: Fuseworks advises using their glass for certain results; however, over the past two years, I've been experimenting with a wide range of different kinds of glass pieces (along with theirs), and all types have yielded good results.

Here are my findings. There are stores that specialize in mosaics and glass fusing and they'll sell glass that you can use in this kiln. A COE (Coefficient of Expansion, or how quickly the glass cools) of 90 is primarily what is used and what is recommended for this kiln. However, glass comes in all kinds of different COEs. Mixing COEs will cause the glass pieces you make to crack and break, because some parts will cool faster than others. Have you ever filled a hot glass from the dishwasher with cold water? It can be scary.

I've found that if you use glass marbles from the same bag, they work well together. Often glass pieces from the same company will work well together. You just have to experiment and keep your glass pieces together. For example, decorative glass chips from the craft store, if they're all made by the same company, generally have the same COE and can work well together in the kiln. Pieces of the same broken bottle can work well, too. You can always try mixing different pieces if you don't know the exact COE and risk cracking and breakage, though much of the time I've had good luck finding glass pieces that work well together in the kiln.

I've also found that using small amounts of glass beads creates a nice effect on glass and the beads don't cause the piece to crack. You'll see that I sprinkled black bugle beads on a few pieces in this chapter, and they look amazing. Really, it's all about experimentation and keeping track of your findings. Most important, though, is SAFETY!

# FUSED GLASS AND CHAIN

As I've mentioned, I've been going crazy making glass pieces. Not your typical fused glass pieces, but what I like to call "glass gems." I was lucky enough to find some very dark red glass and mixed it with these pieces for a shot of color. Find a glass store in your area that works with stained glass, and you'll be well on your way to experimenting with all different techniques.

## YoU'LL NeED

- ◆ Fuseworks Microwave Kiln Kit (see Resource Guide)
- ◆ Fuse paper (usually included in the kiln kit)
- ◆ Clear flat glass marbles (you can often find bags of them at the dollar store in the flower-arranging area)
- ◆ Black glass beads
- ◆ Red glass chips
- ◆ Elmer's Glue-All
- ◆ E-6000 glue
- ◆ Aluminum flashing
- ◆ Tin shears or heavy-duty scissors with serrated blades
- ◆ Scrap wood
- ◆ Drill with small drill bit
- ◆ 3 feet of medium silver-tone chain
- ◆ 1 silver-tone lobster claw closure
- ◆ 6 silver-tone jump rings
- ◆ Piece of scrap wood
- ◆ Needle-nose pliers (and wirecutters if the pliers don't have them)

# HeRE's HoW

1. With your Elmer's Glue-All, glue some black glass beads and some red glass chips on the center of a clear glass flat marble, place on your fuse paper on the base of your kiln, and microwave in the kiln on high for three to four minutes, depending on your microwave (see tips on page 139). Create five different gems, making sure to use the same technique each time to get similar results.

2. Let your pieces cool after you use your kiln each time.

3. Pick three fused glass gems and decide how you want to position them on the aluminum flashing. (These will be the three connected pieces.) With tin shears or heavy-duty serrated scissors, cut a piece of flashing 4 inches by 8 inches. Trace the rough shapes onto the flashing, leaving enough space around each piece to accommodate the chain.

4. Cut out your aluminum piece, glue down your three fused glass gems, and let dry.

5. Repeat the same process for the two remaining glass gems, but cut out the circles from the flashing completely; these will hang down from the main piece.

6. With a toothpick and your E-6000, glue chain around your glass pieces, and let dry.

7. Drill a hole on each side of your three-piece component by placing the drill inside one of the chain links. Do this on top of some scrap wood so you don't ruin a surface.

8. Drill a hole in the bottom center of your three-piece component.

9. Drill two holes opposite from each other on your dangling pieces and one hole on the other dangling piece.

10. Attach all the pieces together with jump rings.

11. Add 8 inches of chain on each side of your three-piece component with two more jump rings.

12. Add two jump rings to the ends of the chain and a lobster claw for the closure.

# FUSED GLASS AND METAL CUFF

This piece looks expensive and artsy. It's just the kind of piece you could wear to a chic gallery opening. When they find out you made it yourself, it'll be YOU everyone's talking about. I guarantee it!

## YOU'LL NEED

- Large piece of fused glass
  (see instructions and materials on page 139)
- Flat metal cuff
- Aluminum flashing
- Tin shears or heavy-duty scissors with
  serrated blades
- Scrap wood
- E-6000 glue
- Krylon silver metallic
- Krylon gray primer

## HERE'S HOW

**1** With tin shears or heavy-duty serrated
scissors, cut a piece of aluminum flashing
4 inches by 4 inches. Trace around your piece
of fused glass on the aluminum flashing. Add
an extra border of about ⅛ inch to the tracings
and cut out that shape from the flashing.

**2** Glue the aluminum shape to the metal cuff
with E-6000 and let dry.

**3** Spray the entire cuff with the gray primer and
let dry.

**4** Spray the cuff with the metallic silver and let
dry.

**5** Glue on the piece of fused glass with more
E-6000 and let dry.

# FUSED GLASS DOUBLE BROOCH

Why not have two instead of one? This way you can wear this brooch all sorts of different ways! Perhaps you could use it to keep a chic scarf around your neck or even use it like an old sweater clip to keep your cardigan from falling off. Either way, as I always say, two is better than one.

## YOU'LL NEED

- 2 pieces of fused glass (see instructions and materials on page 139)
- Aluminum flashing
- Tin shears or heavy-duty scissors with serrated blades
- Scrap wood
- Hammer and small nail
- Piece of scrap wood
- E-6000 glue
- 25 inches of fine silver-tone chain
- 2 silver-tone jump rings
- 2 pin backs (see Resource Guide)
- *Optional:* Drill with very small drill bit

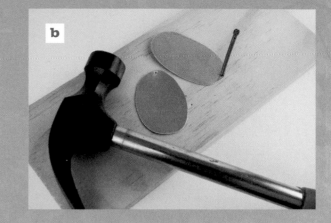

## HeRE's HoW

1. With tin shears or heavy-duty serrated scissors, cut out a piece of aluminum flashing 4 inches by 4 inches. Trace around each fused glass piece on the aluminum flashing.

2. Add an extra border to the tracings the width of your chain and cut out the shapes from the flashing.

3. On a piece of scrap wood to protect your work surface, tap a hole through one end of each piece of flashing with your hammer and nail. (Or you could use a drill with a very small drill bit.)

4. Flip the pieces over and tap the hole with the hammer to eliminate any sharp edges.

5. Glue the fused glass pieces to the flashing pieces with E-6000, making sure not to cover the holes, and let dry.

6. Cut four lengths of chain: 5 inches, 4½ inches, 4 inches, and 3½ inches. Connect the ends of the chains together with jump rings and then attach the jump rings to the holes in the flashing.

7. Glue your pin backs on the flashing and let dry.

# FUSED GLASS COCKTAIL EARRINGS

Sometimes I call my friends and tell them to dress up in their finest outfits so we can go out to dinner. It doesn't matter where we go, it's just fun to dress up and look wonderful. Why have fancy jewelry and clothes if you only wear them once a year? No one has to know that you're not coming from the opera or a swanky event, right? I think these earrings are going to make an appearance (on my friend Kelly) at our next fancy outing.

## You'll Need

- Four pieces of fused glass (see instructions and materials on page 139)
- Aluminum flashing
- Tin shears or heavy-duty scissors with serrated blades
- Scrap wood
- E-6000 glue
- 12 inches of crystal chain
- 2 silver-tone clip-on earring blanks
- 6 silver-tone jump rings
- Needle-nose pliers (and wirecutters if the pliers don't have them)

## Here's How

1. With tin shears or heavy-duty scissors, cut a piece from the aluminum flashing 4 inches by 4 inches. Place your fused glass pieces on the flashing and carefully trace around them.

2. Add a border the width of your crystal chain to your tracings on the aluminum flashing and cut the pieces out.

3. Glue your glass pieces on the flashing with E-6000, and let dry.

4. Glue one jump ring to the edge of each piece with a dab of E-6000.

5. Circle your glass pieces with the crystal chain to determine how long the chain needs to be. Cut the chain to size. With dabs of E-6000 on a toothpick, glue the chain around each piece, and let dry.

6. Link the two pieces together with another jump ring.

7. Glue a clip-on earring blank to the back of each piece, and let dry.

# FUSED GLASS COCKTAIL RING

Nothing says glamour like a big cocktail ring. Fused glass pieces are the perfect stone for this project, and there are as many variations as there are snowflakes. Just fuse your glass piece in the colors you like to create your gem and you're halfway there.

## YOU'LL NEED

- Fused glass piece (see instructions and materials on page 139)
- Enough crystal chain to encircle the piece of glass
- E-6000 glue
- Toothpicks
- Aluminum flashing
- Tin shears or heavy-duty scissors with serrated blades
- Scrap wood
- Ring blank

## HERE'S HOW

1. With tin shears or heavy-duty serrated scissors, cut out a small square (a couple of inches square should be enough) from the aluminum flashing. Trace around your fused glass gem with a fine marker on the flashing.

2. Add a border the width of your crystal chain to your tracings on the aluminum flashing and cut the pieces out.

3. Carefully cut out your shape.

4. Glue the glass gem in the center of the flashing with E-6000. With dabs of E-6000 on a toothpick, carefully glue the crystal chain around the perimeter, and let dry.

5. Glue a ring blank on the back with a generous gob of E-6000, and let dry. Now get out there and knock 'em dead!

# FUSED GLASS CHECKERBOARD GEMS

This was a real challenge to make, but once I figured it out, it was smooth sailing!
My best creative advice is to just go for it! What is the worst that could happen? It's
just a craft project, right?

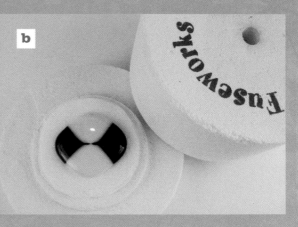

## YOU'LL NEED

- ◆ Fuseworks Microwave Kiln Kit (see Resource Guide)
- ◆ Fuse paper (usually included in the kiln kit)
- ◆ 10 white marbles
- ◆ 10 black marbles
- ◆ E-6000 glue
- ◆ Elmer's Glue-All
- ◆ Wax paper
- ◆ Cardboard
- ◆ 36 inches of medium silver-tone chain
- ◆ 18 inches of large silver-tone chain
- ◆ 2 three- or four-strand clasp ends (I used a four-strand because the large chain was too big for a three-strand.)
- ◆ Aluminum flashing
- ◆ Tin shears or heavy-duty scissors with serrated blades
- ◆ Scrap wood
- ◆ 10 silver-tone jump rings
- ◆ 1 large silver-tone lobster claw closure
- ◆ Needle-nose pliers (and wirecutters if the pliers don't have them)
- ◆ Elmer's Glue-All

## HERE'S HOW

**1** With Elmer's glue, glue together two white and two black marbles, as seen in photo a, on fuse paper on the base of your microwave kiln and let dry for a few minutes.

**2** Microwave for about four minutes on high to fuse them, as seen in photo b. You will need to experiment because each microwave kiln is different. It may take four and a half minutes in yours (see tips on page 139). This is the fun part!

**3** Repeat steps 1 and 2 until you have created five checkerboard gems.

**4** Lay down a sheet of wax paper on cardboard.

**5** Cut 36 inches of medium chain and 18 inches of large chain. Lay them down on the wax paper in the curved shape of the choker, as seen in photo c. This is very important! The chains must be in the shape of the choker or it won't lie properly on your neck.

**6** With a generous amount of E-6000, glue your checkerboard gems in place on the curved chains and let dry. Make sure to get the glue on all three chains and don't move them until all of the pieces are completely dry.

**7** With tin shears or heavy-duty serrated scissors, cut five small circles from the flashing a bit smaller than your fused glass pieces.

**8** When the glass pieces are dry on the chain, glue an aluminum circle to the back of each gem. This will hide the glue gobs and keep the inside neat.

**9** Cut your chains so that they are all the same length at the back and add them to the clasp ends with jump rings.

**10** Add another jump ring and a lobster claw for the closure.

# BRASS AND GLASS COCKTAIL RINGS

A bold cocktail ring is the easiest go-to accessory to pull off, and these are just the ticket to make something as simple as a pair of jeans and a T-shirt look amazing. I haven't been able to keep these around long enough to photograph them, because my female friends have been snagging them! I think they're a hit.

## YOU'LL NEED

- Fuseworks Microwave Kiln Kit (see Resource Guide)
- Fuse paper (usually included in the kiln kit)
- A fused glass piece (see instruction and materials on page 139) for each ring you want to make
- E-6000 glue
- Needle-nose pliers
- Ring blanks
- Various stamped brass ornaments

## HeRE's HoW

1. Glue your glass pieces together with the Elmer's and then fuse them in the Fuseworks Microwave Kiln Kit according to the instructions included with the kit and let cool (see tips on page 139).

2. Remove the fuse paper from the back.

3. Figure out which stamped brass piece you want to use for your ring and see if it fits on the glass. You may have to bend a little piece like a leg or wing down on the edges. It's easy, just use pliers.

4. With a generous glob of E-6000, glue your brass ornament on the fused glass and let dry.

5. Turn your piece over, glue on your ring blank with more E-6000, and let dry.

> **Hint:**
> You can order brass stampings and ring blanks online at www.bsueboutiques.com OR www.vintagejewelrysupplies.com. Both places have LOVELY selections.

# CAGED GEMS

I have a superstition about book writing. The first project I finish for a book has to be amazing . . . at least to me. So, without further ado, here it is, my Caged Gem Necklace made from some of my favorite fused glass pieces. I like wrapping things in wire, but not always in the usual ways. Using wire to secure the gems seemed like a nice break from the everyday wire-wrapping projects (although that technique would work well for this, too).

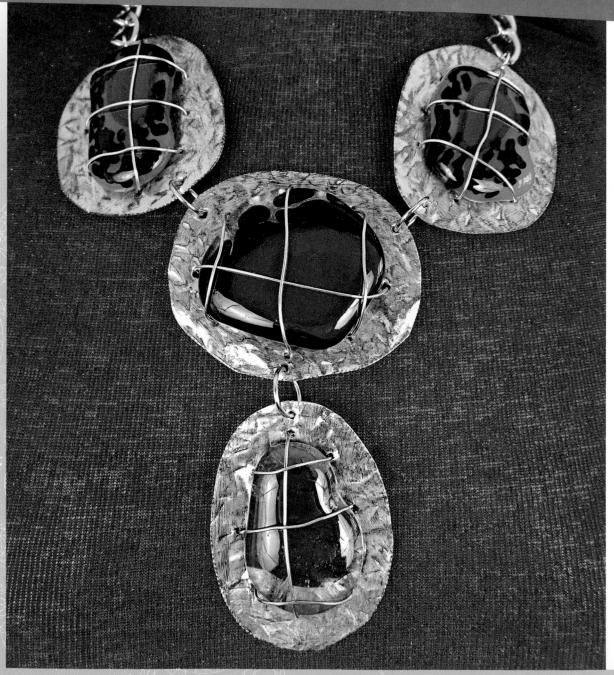

## You'll Need

- Piece of aluminum flashing
- Tin shears or heavy-duty scissors with serrated blades
- Scrap wood
- 4 large pieces of fused glass (see instructions and materials on page 139) or paper turquoise stones (see instructions and materials on page 74)
- 5 large silver-tone jump rings
- 2 pieces of large silver-tone chain, each 6 inches long
- 1 silver-tone lobster claw closure
- Hammer and nail
- Piece of scrap wood
- Lumiere metallic paint in pewter
- Rags
- 60 inches of 20-gauge wire
- Needle-nose pliers (and wirecutters if the pliers don't have them)
- Minwax Clear Brushing Lacquer
- Small paintbrush

## Here's How

1. Using tin shears or heavy-duty serrated scissors, cut a piece of aluminum flashing 6 inches by 8 inches. Trace the rough shape of your fused glass pieces onto the flashing. Cut four ovals from the flashing ⅜ inch to ½ inch larger than your glass pieces (or paper turquoise stones) all the way around.

2. Place an aluminum oval on your scrap wood and hammer it until it has a nice texture. Repeat for the others.

3. With a rag, rub on the Lumiere pewter paint and let dry. Make sure it is applied evenly and gets into all the cracks and folds.

4. Coat each piece with Minwax Clear Brushing Lacquer.

5. Place your fused glass gems on each oval and mark spots for eight holes, evenly spaced around the gems.

6. Tap the holes in the ovals with your hammer and nail. Use your scrap wood to protect your countertop or work surface.

7. Flip the ovals over and tap the holes to make sure there are no sharp edges.

8. Thread the wire back and forth through the holes to secure the stone on top of the oval. If you want to glue the stones on the oval first, that's fine.

9. Figure out the placement of your ovals for the necklace, and on three of them, make holes in opposite ends of the oval. On one of those three you will make a third hole from which to hang your fourth piece. On the fourth piece you will need to make only one hole.

10. Attach your pieces with large jump rings.

11. Attach your chains to the end pieces.

12. Attach jump rings and your lobster claw to the ends of the chains for the closure.

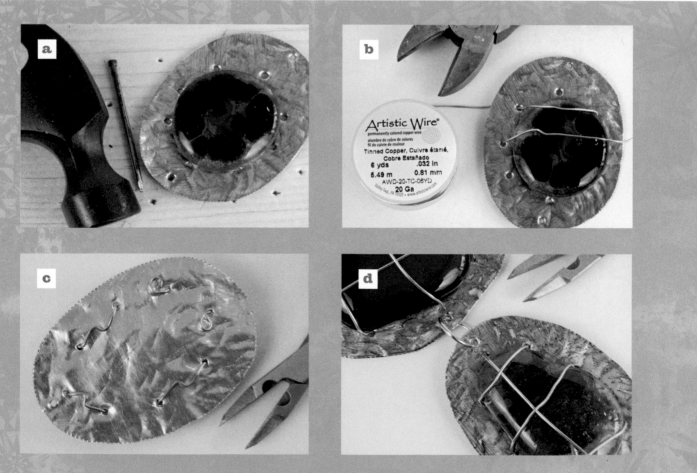

## YOU'LL NEED

- Aluminum flashing
- Scrap wood
- 1 piece of fused glass (see instructions and materials on page 139)
- Tin shears or heavy-duty scissors with serrated blades
- Silver-tone ring blank
- E-6000 glue
- Hammer and nail
- Piece of scrap wood
- Lumiere metallic paint in pewter
- Rags
- 15 inches of 20-gauge wire
- Needle-nose pliers (and wirecutters if the pliers don't have them)
- Minwax Clear Brushing Lacquer
- Small paintbrush
- Ring blank

# CAGED GLASS COCKTAIL RING

## HERE'S HOW

1. With tin shears or heavy-duty serrated scissors, cut a piece of aluminum flashing 2 inches by 3 inches. Cut an oval from the flashing that is ⅜ inch to ½ inch larger than your fused glass piece all the way around.

2. Place the oval on your scrap wood and hammer it until it has a nice texture.

3. With a rag, rub on the Lumiere pewter paint and let it dry. Make sure it is applied evenly and gets in all the cracks and folds.

4. Coat the oval with Minwax Clear Brushing Lacquer.

5. Place your fused glass gem on the oval and mark spots for eight holes, evenly spaced around the gem.

6. Tap the holes in the oval with your hammer and nail. Use your scrap wood to protect your countertop or work surface.

7. Flip it over and tap the holes to make sure there are no sharp edges.

8. Thread wire back and forth through the holes to secure the stone on top of the oval. If you want to glue the stone on the oval first, that's okay, too.

9. With a generous amount of E-6000, adhere fused glass gem to the ring blank and let dry.

# GLASS, METAL, TWINE

There are times when you just have to experiment without caring about the results. It helps push you to different places and get you out of your creative routine. This bracelet did just that. It doesn't use a color scheme or even shapes that I tend to gravitate toward. I do happen to love where I ended up with it, though. Toss a few things together and see what happens. You just might surprise yourself.

## YOU'LL NEED

- Aluminum flashing
- Scrap wood
- 3 fused glass pieces (see instructions and materials on page 139) or large beads
- E-6000 glue
- Paintbrushes
- Colored twine in a color you like (I used bright yellow)
- Tin shears or heavy-duty scissors with serrated blades
- Piece of scrap wood
- Hammer and nail
- Bright blue and bright green acrylic paint
- Rags
- Small paintbrush
- Minwax Polycrylic clear coat
- 10 silver-tone jump rings
- 2 to 3 inches of large silver-tone link chain
- Needle-nose pliers *(and wirecutters if the pliers don't have them)*
- 3 inches of medium silver-tone link chain
- 1 silver-tone lobster claw closure

## HERE'S HOW

1. With tin shears or heavy-duty serrated scissors, cut three rectangles from the aluminum flashing, each 3 inches by 1½ inches.

2. On top of a piece of scrap wood tap the flashing pieces with the hammer to give them a hammered texture.

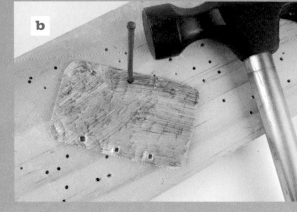

3. Rub blue paint into each piece with a rag and let dry.

4. On two of the rectangles, tap three evenly spaced holes on one 3-inch side, and one hole in the center of the other 3-inch side.

5. On the third rectangle, tap three holes on each of the 3-inch sides. This is your center rectangle.

6. Flip each piece over and gently tap the holes to eliminate any sharp edges.

7. With a brush, paint around the edges of each rectangle in green and let dry.

8. Brush the three rectangles with Minwax Polycrylic to coat them.

9. Glue a fused glass stone in the center of each of the rectangles with E-6000.

10. Using a toothpick to spread E-6000 around the edge of your glass pieces, add twine around each one.

11. Use your needle-nose pliers to connect the rectangles together on the three-hole sides with jump rings.

12. Add the large links of chain to each end of the rectangles with another jump ring.

13. Add the smaller chain to one side with another jump ring and another jump ring with a lobster claw to the other end for the closure.

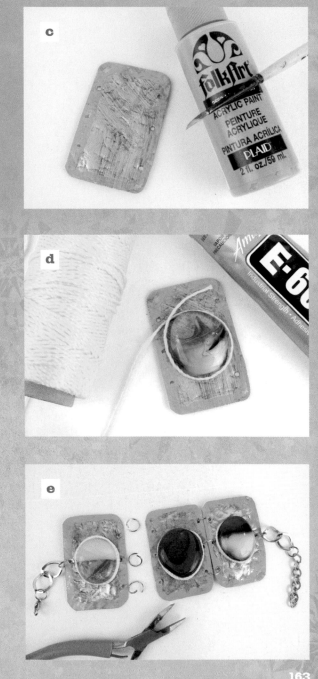

**P**retty soon I'm just going to have to own up to the fact that I'm really just a large (albeit hairy) child. I like toys, anything shiny and colorful, and dolls. Okay, creepy dolls, but I do like them. As much as I thought I would outgrow these interests, I never have. There is something to say for embracing your inner child. That's what I've done with the projects on these next few pages. They may use elements that kids would love, but it doesn't mean you can't love them, too!

# KOLORFUL KID COUTURE

I got a huge bottle of these plastic Melty Beads (also called Perler Beads) at IKEA years ago, and I just love them. They remind me of my trip to Africa and all the beautiful colors that were mixed together in the art and accessories I saw there. This project is perfect for kids, but I bet you'll enjoy it just as much as I did. Try using only one or two colors instead of all of them. Maybe just red and blue, or yellow and orange. It's really up to you. Just have fun!

## YOU'LL NEED

- Bottle or bag of Melty Beads or Perler beads (www.createforless.com has a terrific selection)
- Tons of 5-inch-long nylon zip ties
- Scissors
- Black chain (or any color you like) with large links
  - 10 inches for each long necklace
  - 8 inches for each choker
- Needle-nose pliers (and wirecutters if the pliers don't have them)
- 1 lobster claw closure for the short choker and for each bracelet
- 2 large jump rings for the short choker and for each bracelet

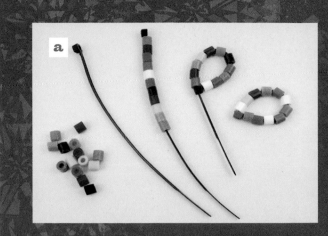

## HERE'S HOW

### FOR THE LONG NECKLACE

1. Create several links by stringing 11 beads on each nylon tie and then zipping them closed.
2. Carefully cut off the excess.
3. String your beads on another tie and loop it through the first and then zip it closed again. See, you're creating a chain already!
4. Create chains that are about 27 to 31 links long, depending on how long you want your necklaces.
5. Add your last links through the end link on the 10-inch piece of large link chain.
6. Do the same on the other end to finish.

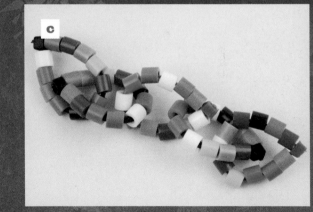

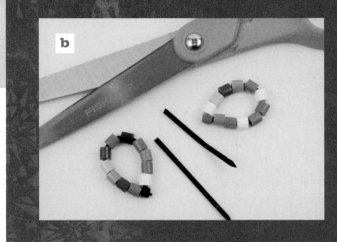

### FOR THE SHORTER CHOKER

1. Follow the steps above but only use one color per link.
2. Create three link chains that are seven, nine, and eleven links long.
3. Cut your large link chain into two 4-inch pieces.
4. Add all three beaded links to one more link and add that one link to the chain.
5. Do the same on the other side.
6. Add jump rings and a lobster claw to the ends for the closure.

# FOR THE BRACELETS

**1** Follow steps 1 through 3 for the necklace, but create only as many links as will wrap around your wrist.

**2** Add an extra-large jump ring and lobster claw to the ends for a closure.

# WOW HEADBAND

I cannot stop buying magnetic letters at the dollar store. They are just too much fun to have on the fridge and use for craft projects. This headband is a terrific project for a bachelorette or birthday party. Whatever the occasion, spell it out and wear it proudly on top of your head!

## YoU'LL NeED

- Enough magnetic letters to spell your word
- E-6000 glue
- Wax paper
- Fine sandpaper
- Plastic headband
- Krylon Fusion for Plastic in pink or purple
- Krylon Glitter Blast in Posh Pink
- Feathers
- Hot glue gun and glue sticks

## HeRE's HoW

**1** On a sheet of wax paper, lay out your letters above the headband so you know the placement. IMPORTANT! Make sure they are spaced far enough apart so that when you open the headband to put it on your head, the letters don't squish together and pop off!

**2** Sand the edges of your letters and the headband where you will be gluing them together. This will give the glue some tooth and keep bond sturdy.

**3** Apply a generous dollop (but be neat!) of E-6000 glue on the bottom of each letter where it touches the headband. The glue will not stick to the wax paper.

**4** When the letters are dry, spray them with a base coat of Krylon Fusion for Plastic.

**5** Spray the Glitter Blast on the headband and let dry.

**6** Hot-glue feathers on the back of one of the letters.

# I HEART YOU KATY PERRY!

I have a crush on Katy Perry. Maybe it's because she wears a blue wig or that her dresses always look like cupcakes and glitter? I don't know! I just adore her. My crush inspired me to make this heart necklace, which I'm planning to send to her. Katy, if you're reading this between concerts, please send me your shipping address.

Love, Mark.

## YOU'LL NEED

- Flat, thin cardboard
- Elmer's Glue-All
- 3D Crystal Lacquer (www.sakuracraft.com)
- Flat-back acrylic gems in different colors, shapes, and sizes
- 1 yard of crystal chain
- Needle-nose pliers (and wirecutters if the pliers don't have them)
- 20 inches of ¼-inch turquoise blue grosgrain (ribbed) ribbon
- 20 inches of 1-inch pink grosgrain ribbon
- 10 inches of ¼-inch red satin ribbon
- E-6000 glue
- Toothpicks
- Hot glue gun and glue sticks
- Loose silver glitter
- Sequins

## HeRE's How

1. Cut a heart out of your cardboard about 3 inches wide.

2. Spread a layer of Elmer's glue on top of the entire heart and quickly place your gems and sequins on the heart.

3. Sprinkle the loose glitter over the gems and add more glue and glitter where needed.

4. When dry, use dabs of E-6000 on a toothpick and carefully glue your crystal chain around the outer edge of the heart.

5. When the heart is completely dry, apply a coat of 3D Crystal Lacquer to keep the glitter in place and keep it from flaking. It dries quickly.

6. Cut 14 inches of crystal chain. Lay your turquoise ribbon flat and with E-6000 on a toothpick, glue the chain along the ribbon.

7. Cut two 4-inch pieces of crystal chain. Lay your pink ribbon flat, and using a toothpick and E-6000, glue gems and 4 inches of crystal chain on each side of your ribbon, leaving a blank space in the center.

8. Fold your red ribbon in half and hot-glue it to the back of the heart.

9. Tie the red ribbon around the center of the turquoise and pink ribbon and then tie it in a bow.

10. Use the extra ribbon at the back to tie a bow for the closure.

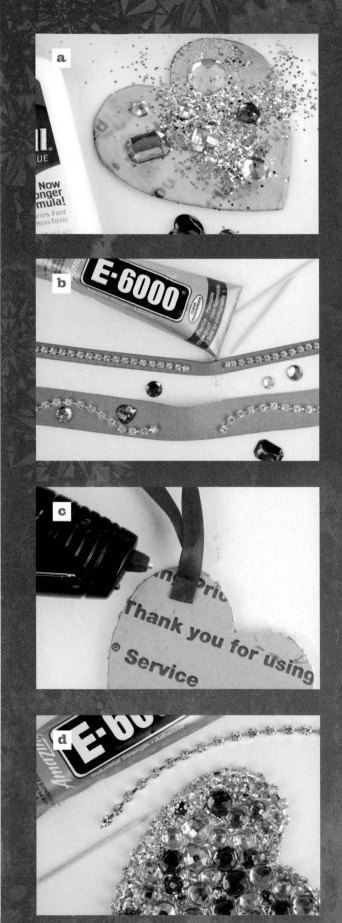

# NOIR DRAMATIQUE

I got a little French when I was naming this project because Zip Tie Choker just didn't capture how dramatic it looked. Besides, when something has a terrific name, it just seems more impressive, don't you think? For example, if you name your child Hercules or Superman, they are instantly interesting. If you name them, oh, I don't know, something like MARK, they have to work a lot harder to create that mystique. So, Noir Dramatique it is!

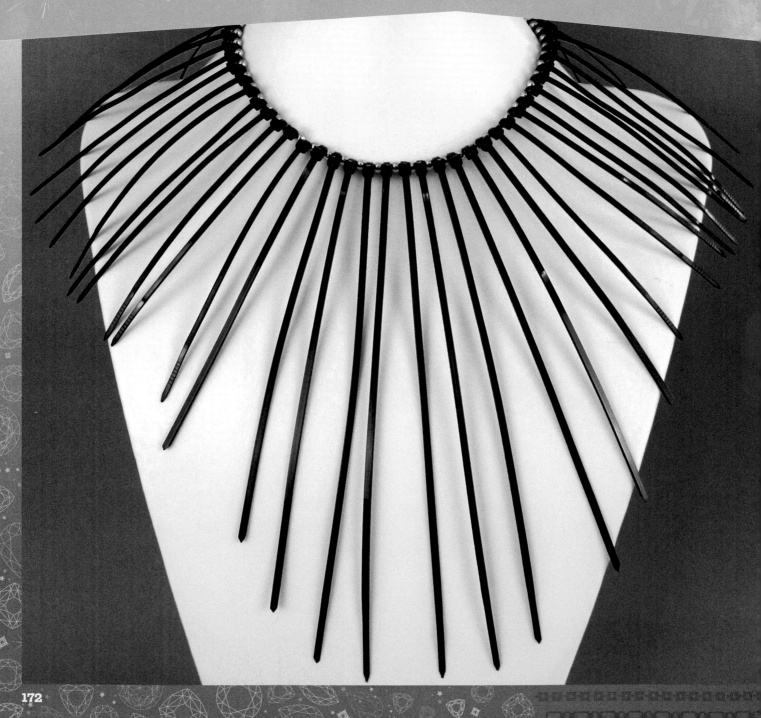

## YOU'LL NEED

- Beading wire and crimping beads
- Needle-nose pliers (and wirecutters if the pliers don't have them)
- 57 gold beads
- 22 (3-inch) black zip ties
- 22 (4-inch) black zip ties
- 11 (7-inch) black zip ties
- 1 gold-tone lobster claw closure
- 1 gold-tone jump ring

## HERE'S HOW

1. Close all your zip ties, leaving only a small hole at the ends. This turns it into a bead with a very long tail.

2. Cut off about 16 inches of beading wire and string a crimping bead onto it, followed by the lobster claw.

3. Put the end of the beading wire back through your crimping bead and crimp it with your needle-nose pliers.

4. Start with a gold bead and then alternate 11 of your 3-inch zip ties and gold beads.

5. Continue with gold beads and 11 of the 4-inch zip ties, then 11 of the 7-inch zip ties, then 11 of the 4-inch zip ties, and finally 11 of the 3-inch zip ties.

6. Repeat the crimping process from step 2 on a jump ring to close the choker.

7. Leaving the three longest center zip ties alone, trim the four 7-inch zip ties on each side of the center ties so they graduate from short to long as shown in photo d.

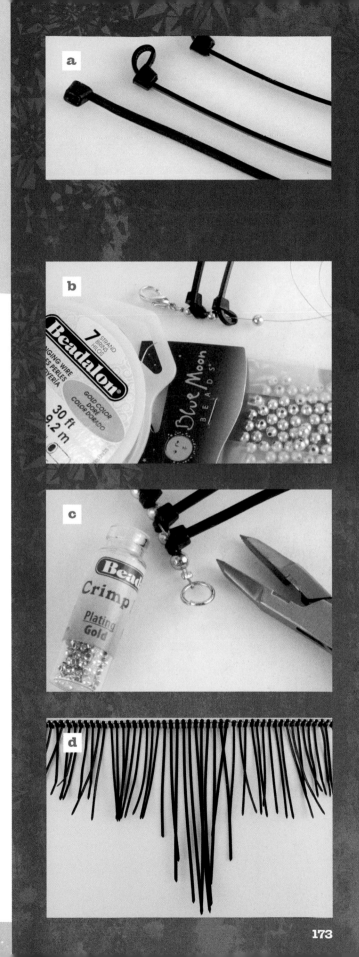

# BELLE OF THE PING-PONG BALL

I can already hear the telephone ringing and Betty Draper from *Mad Men* asking me if she can borrow this piece for her next fund-raiser. Who ever thought Ping-Pong balls could be so chic?

## YoU'LL NeeD

- 3 Ping-Pong balls
- Hot glue gun and glue sticks
- Two-tone decorative (or plain) twine
- 4 gold beads for spacers
- 12 inches of large gold-tone chain (www.createforless.com has a great selection of chain)
- 4 gold-tone jump rings
- 1 gold-tone lobster claw closure
- Gold-tone beading wire
- Gold-tone crimp beads
- Needle-nose pliers (and wirecutters if the pliers don't have them)
- Scissors
- Large pin

## HeRE's HoW

**1** With dabs of hot glue, wind and wrap your Ping-Pong ball with the twine, starting at the base and moving upward, until the entire ball is covered. This technique might take a little getting used to, but once you get the hang of it, you'll be fine.

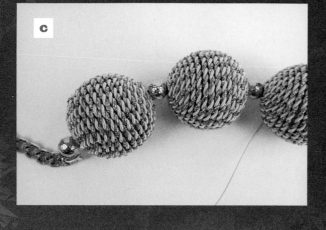

**2** Poke holes in two opposite ends of the ball (where you started and finished wrapping the twine) with a large pin.

**3** Cut 12 inches of beading wire, place a crimp bead on the end, wrap the wire around a jump ring and then back through the crimp bead, and then crimp with your needle-nose pliers.

**4** Thread your beads and balls and finish by crimping the end of the wire around another jump ring.

**5** Cut two 6-inch pieces of chain. Add jump rings to the ends of the chains and attach on both sides of the choker and a lobster claw for the closure.

# HARAJUKU HEADBAND

Eat your heart out, Gwen Stefani! Your Harajuku girls are already loving this!

## You'll Need

- ◆ 2 Ping-Pong balls
- ◆ 1 plastic headband
- ◆ Hot glue gun and glue sticks
- ◆ Two-tone decorative (or plain) twine

## Here's How

**1** With dabs of hot glue, wind and wrap your Ping-Pong ball with the twine, starting at the base and moving upward, until the entire ball is covered. This technique might take a little getting used to, but once you get the hang of it, you'll be fine.

**2** Dab the hot glue on the end of the plastic headband and wrap it all the way to the other end, making sure to use dabs of hot glue all along the headband as you wrap.

**3** Using a generous amount of hot glue, secure the balls on top of the headband and let dry.

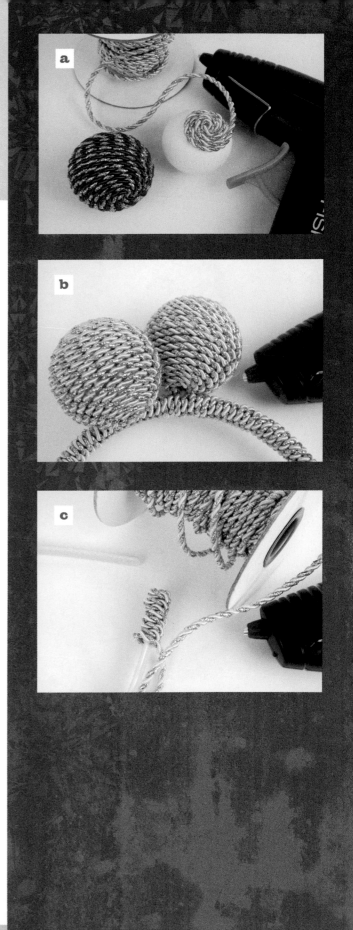

## SEXY AND THE CITY

Just like Carrie Bradshaw, you can wear your name (or whatever you like) around your neck and make your statement! Though this is not a very subtle piece of jewelry to wear, it certainly is fun. Even though I used kids' toys for this necklace, save this Carrie-inspired piece for the grown-ups!

## You'll Need

- Plastic magnet letter sets from the dollar store
- Wax paper
- E-6000 glue
- Large safety pin
- Tealight
- Needle-nose pliers (and wirecutters if the pliers don't have them)
- 12 inches of silver-tone chain
- 4 silver-tone jump rings

## Here's How

**1** Glue your letters together side by side on some wax paper with E-6000 and let dry.

**2** Hold the safety pin with pliers and heat it with the tealight. Carefully poke a hole in the outer edge of each of the two end letters. These will be for your jump rings, so make sure the holes are big enough for a jump ring to fit.

**3** Cut the chain into two 6-inch pieces. Attach jump rings to the end letters and attach a piece of chain from each jump ring.

**4** Attach jump rings and a lobster claw to the ends of the chains for the closure.

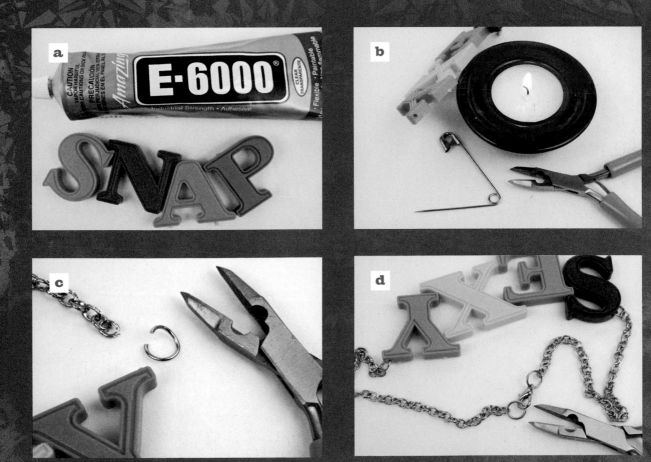

# ZAMBIA!

Not only could ZAMBIA! be the name of a Broadway show that Julie Tamor would direct, but it also fills me with images of vibrant colors and tribal drum beats. I think it perfectly describes this piece.

## YOU'LL NEED

- 23 large zip ties
- Perler beads in various colors (www.createforless.com has a terrific selection)
- E-6000 glue
- Scissors
- 9 inches of black chain
- Crimp beads
- 2 silver-tone jump rings
- 1 silver-tone lobster claw closure
- 18 inches of silver beading wire
- Needle-nose pliers (and wirecutters if the pliers don't have them)

The perfect thing about large nylon zip ties is that the Perler beads fit on them perfectly without moving. If by chance the beads *do* move when you put them on the zip ties, dab some E-6000 at the base to keep them in place.

## HERE'S HOW

**1** Create loops at the end of each of your 23 zip ties by closing the zip ties, leaving only a small hole at the ends.

**2** String 10 beads each on 6 of the nylon ties.

**3** String 15 beads on 6 of the nylon ties.

**4** String 19 beads on 6 of the nylon ties.

**5** String 21 beads on 5 of the nylon ties.

**6** Cut two 4½-inch pieces of black chain. Place the beading wire and a crimping bead on the end link of one of your 4½-inch pieces of black chain. Your beading wire should be 15 to 17 inches long depending on the size of your neck.

**7** Thread the beaded nylon ties in this order with a bead in between each nylon tie:
3 ties with 10 beads
3 ties with 15 beads
3 ties with 19 beads
5 ties with 21 beads
3 ties with 19 beads
3 ties with 15 beads
3 ties with 10 beads

**8** Finish off your string of beaded nylon ties by looping the end of the beading wire over the end loop of your other 4½-inch piece of black chain and using a crimping bead to secure it.

**9** Add jump rings to the end of each chain and a lobster claw for the closure.

**10** Trim the zip ties so that they graduate in length, with the longest strands in the middle.

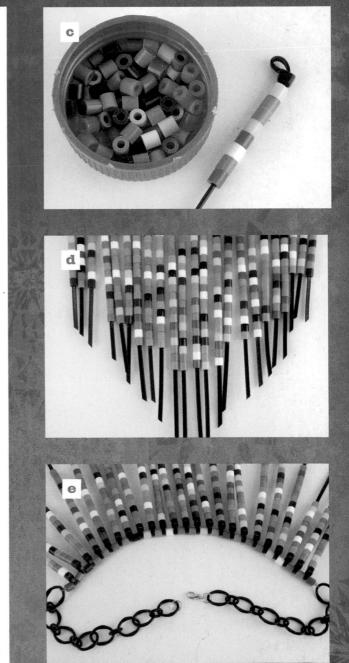

'll admit it, I'm a hoarder! When I hit the dollar store, I stock up on things that I may or may not use right away. In my haul there are always packages of bobby pins and safety pins because I know that one day I WILL use them! That day has finally arrived! Bobby pins and safety pins make up the projects in this chapter, and I've done my best to use them in ways that are a little bit different. My favorite pieces are the Starbursts (pages 186–190) and Bobby's Red Gem Necklace and Earrings (page 202). I know you'll be able to take these ideas even further and make them your own. When you do, make sure you send me a shout-out and share with me what you made. I'm proud of you already!

# BOBBIES AND CHAINS

I think today is the day you should challenge yourself to make something amazing out of an ordinary object. Things like bobby pins, paper clips, and simple chains can become amazing pieces of jewelry if you use your imagination and just go for it. I'm constantly on a quest for new ways to use common things. Any bit of chain you have hanging around your craft bin will work for this project.

## YOU'LL NEED

- 12 inches of heavy-gauge wire that doesn't bend easily
- Needle-nose pliers (and wirecutters if the pliers don't have them)
- 2 yards of various chains in silver and gold tones and in different sizes
- 95 bobby pins
- 24 inches of medium silver-tone chain
- About 20 silver- or gold-tone jump rings
- 1 silver- or gold-tone lobster claw

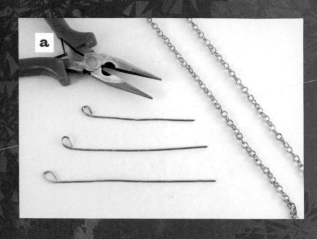

## HERE'S HOW

**1** Cut your wire into three pieces: 4 inches, 3½ inches, and 3 inches. Bend loops on one side of each piece with your needle-nose pliers.

**2** Cut the medium silver chain into two 12-inch pieces. Thread the 4-inch wire through the bottom link of one of the 12-inch chains.

**3** Place 40 bobby pins on the wire and thread the wire through the bottom link of the other 12-inch chain.

**4** Create another loop with your needle-nose pliers. This will keep it in place.

**5** Working up the necklace, measure above the first row of bobby pins the length of a bobby pin and add ⅜ inch. Thread the 3½-inch wire through the chain.

**6** Repeat steps 3 and 4, adding only 30 bobby pins.

**7** Repeat steps 3, 4, and 5 for your last row of bobby pins, using only 25 bobby pins.

**8** Add jump rings to the ends of your 12-inch pieces of silver chain and a lobster claw for the closure. The top wire is 3 inches long.

**9** With jump rings and your various pieces of extra chain cut into 7- to 12-inch pieces, drape your chains and connect them to the 12-inch side chains, letting the sides of each chain dangle.

**10** Repeat step 9 until you're satisfied with your design.

# STARBURST NECKLACE

I think this actually looks like the key to another dimension. If you were to neatly place the smaller stones, could you perhaps make your astrology sign? Just a thought.

## YoU'LL NeED

- 90 (1½-inch) silver- or gold-tone safety pins
- Aluminum flashing
- Tin shears or heavy-duty scissors with serrated blades
- Scrap wood
- 7 inches of silver or gold medium-gauge wire
- E-6000 glue
- Needle-nose pliers (and wirecutters if the pliers don't have them)
- 1 large flat-back crystal or acrylic gem
- Several small flat-back crystals or acrylic gems
- 15 silver- or gold-tone jump rings
- 22 inches of small to medium gold or silver chain
- 1 silver- or gold-tone lobster claw

## HeRE's HoW

1. Cut a 7-inch piece of the wire. String 60 safety pins on the wire.

2. Bend the wire into a circle, twist the ends together, and cut off the excess, leaving about ½ inch of twisted wire. Tuck this in between the safety pins.

3. With tin shears or heavy-duty serrated scissors, cut a 1½-inch-diameter circle from the aluminum flashing. Glue your starburst of pins on the circle with E-6000 and let dry.

4. Glue the larger gem in the center of the starburst and let dry.

5. Glue the smaller gems in a random design around the starburst.

6. Place a jump ring on the end of one of the safety pins and attach at the center of your chain.

7. Place jump rings on the ends of the chain and a lobster claw for the closure.

8. Place three safety pins on the remaining jump rings and hang them from the bottom of the starburst as shown in photo d. Add the remaining safety pins to the bottom of these to create a fringe effect.

# STARBURST BRACELET

There is something cosmic about this design that reminds me of the '50s.

## YOU'LL NEED

- Aluminum flashing
- Tin shears or heavy-duty scissors with serrated blades
- Scrap wood
- 7 inches of 18- to 20-gauge wire
- Wide flat silver cuff
- 60 (1-inch) silver safety pins
- Needle-nose pliers (and wirecutters if the pliers don't have them)
- E-6000 glue
- 1 large flat-back crystal or acrylic gem

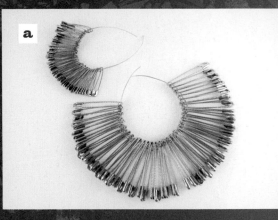

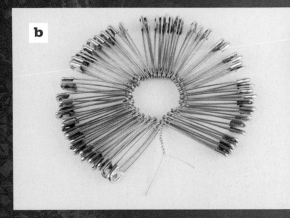

## HeRE's HoW

**1** Cut a 7-inch piece of wire and string the safety pins on it.

**2** Bend the wire into a circle, twist the wire ends together, and cut off the excess, leaving about ½ inch of twisted wire. Tuck this in between the safety pins.

**3** With tin shears or heavy-duty serrated scissors, cut a 1½-inch-diameter circle from the aluminum flashing. Glue your starburst of pins onto the circle with E-6000 and let dry.

**4** Glue your aluminum circle to the center of the metal bracelet with E-6000 and let dry.

**5** Glue your crystal in the center of the starburst and let dry.

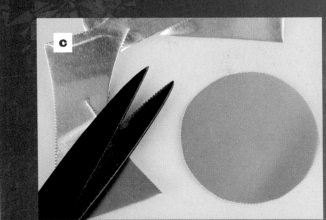

# STARBURST BROOCH: (ODE TO TONY DUQUETTE)

Tony Duquette is one of my all-time favorite artist-designers. He loved dollar stores and using mundane materials to create magical jewelry and enchanting environments. I would stalk him if he were alive today and would have jumped at the chance to work as his assistant (I'd even have done the job for free!). Is there someone who inspires your creativity? If that person is still alive, you must let them know what they mean to you.

## YOU'LL NEED

- 14 inches of medium-gauge wire
- Needle-nose pliers (and wirecutters if the pliers don't have them)
- Aluminum flashing
- Tin shears or heavy-duty scissors with serrated blades
- Scrap wood
- 60 large (no. 3) silver safety pins
- 60 smaller silver safety pins
- 25 gold and silver safety pins in various sizes
- E-6000 glue
- 8 to 10 silver-tone jump rings
- 1 large flat-back crystal or acrylic gem
- Black bugle beads
- Elmer's Glue-All
- Krylon flat black spray paint
- 1 pin back

## HeRE's How

1. Cut a piece of wire 7 inches long. String the 60 large safety pins on.

2. Bend the wire into a circle. Twist the wire to close off the circle, and cut off the extra wire, leaving about ½ inch of twisted wire. Tuck this in between the safety pins.

3. Repeat with the 60 smaller safety pins.

4. With tin shears or heavy-duty serrated scissors, cut a 2-inch-diameter circle from the aluminum flashing.

5. Glue your large starburst on the circle of flashing with E-6000 and let dry.

6. Glue your smaller starburst on top with E-6000 and let dry.

7. Glue your crystal or gem on top of both starbursts and let dry.

8. Smear Elmer's glue all around the edges of the crystal or gem and sprinkle black bugle beads over the glue (as if it were glitter). Reapply glue and bugle beads if you feel you need more. Let dry in place.

9. Carefully spray the ends of the larger starburst of safety pins with the black paint and let dry. You can use any color—I just happen to like the black.

10. Create your safety pin dangler by adding some more bugle beads to the smaller pins and connecting them together and to the bottom of your pin with jump rings.

11. Glue on the pin back with E-6000 and let dry.

# PIN-TASTIC BLINGED-OUT HANDBAG

I know you have an old bag hanging in your closet that you don't know what to do with. Maybe it was a gift from a friend and you're just not in love with it? Well, it's time to give it a makeover and at the same time show the world how crafty you are! Prove that you've got plenty of glamour to spare.

## YOU'LL NEED

- Handbag in need of a makeover
- 1 yard of crystal chain (you can substitute a sparkly brooch here)
- 1 large flat-back crystal or acrylic gem in oval or square
- E-6000 glue
- Toothpicks
- 500 large (no. 3) silver safety pins (hunt around on the Internet to buy in bulk)
- 50 large silver-tone jump rings
- *Optional:* Large-link silver-tone chain (or dog chain from the dollar store) if you need to replace the handle

## HERE'S HOW

### Important!

Your purse will end up looking different from mine. This is a technique that will work on many different kinds of handbags.

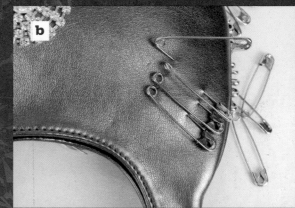

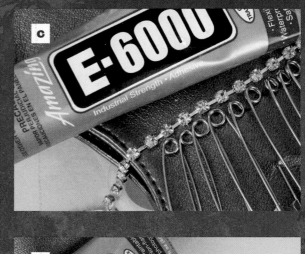

**1** Glue down your large gem in the center of the bag with E-6000 and let dry.

**2** With dabs of E-6000 on a toothpick, start at the edges of the gem, gluing and wrapping the crystal chain around the stone until you have a medallion the size you want in the middle of the bag.

**3** Determine your safety pin design. You can do this on paper first—or just go for it! You can always remove pins if you're not loving them. A good rule of thumb is to start around the edges and work your way in.

**4** Line up your pins evenly as you pin around your bag. This will take a little practice, but it's worth it for speed and accuracy.

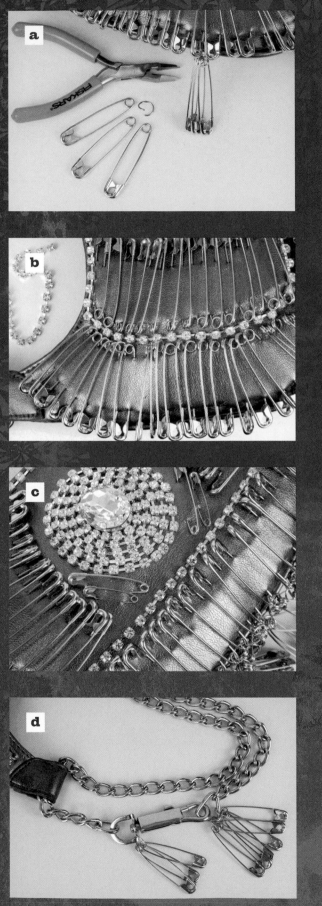

5. Once you have one row of pins fastened to the bag, again with E-6000 on a toothpick, add more crystal chain as you need for your design, and let dry.

6. Continue adding more safety pins until your bag is covered.

7. Add three to five safety pins to a jump ring and add the jump ring to the end of a pin on the bottom of your bag to make the fringe.

8. Continue until you have the length of fringe you want.

9. *Optional:* Replace the handles with dog chain or some large-link chain. There are several ways to do this. You can cut the existing handle, leaving loops to go through the end links of the chain, then glue down the loops with E-6000, secure the bond with clothespins or small clamps, and let dry. If there are already loops that you could attach a chain to, you could just replace the existing handle with your chain.

7

13

# PUNK CHIC DUSTERS

Most punk-inspired jewelry is silver, so I thought, why not give it a golden twist?
Gold safety pins and chain make these dusters superchic.

## YOU'LL NEED

- 2 gold-tone earring wires
- E-6000 glue
- 2 flat eyes from hook and eye set
- 8 inches of crystal chain (I used green)
- 32 inches of small-link gold chain
- 8 gold-tone jump rings
- 16 small gold-tone safety pins
- Needle-nose pliers (and wirecutters if the pliers don't have them)

## HERE'S HOW

1. Cut two 8-inch pieces of crystal chain. Glue your flat eyes on the end crystal of each piece of crystal chain with E-6000 and let dry.

2. Cut eight 4-inch pieces of the small-link gold chain. Place an earring wire, one safety pin, four chains, and crystal chain on a jump ring.

3. Create four additional jump rings filled with three safety pins each and add two to each earring randomly on one of the chains as shown in the photo.

4. Pin one more safety pin through one link of a chain.

# PUNK ROCK SHOWGIRL

Last year I spent New Year's Eve at the Moulin Rouge in Paris watching some very racy French showgirls in outrageously fancy costumes. My favorite part of the show was their attempt at American Pop music, but that's another story! During the performance I got the idea for this showstopper. If I were able to wear it, I'd rock it with a white tank and jeans. Sadly, it just doesn't look that good on me, but I'm sure there's someone out there who can kick up her heels in it!

## YoU'LL NeED

- 130 large (nos. 3 or 4) safety pins
- 140 jump rings
- 50 to 60 sparkly crystal beads
- 3½ yards of chain
- Patience

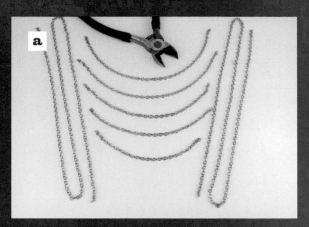

## HeRE's HoW

**1** Cut your chain into seven pieces with the following measurements:
2 pieces 33 inches long (see note below)
1 piece 10 inches
1 piece 9.5 inches
1 piece 8 inches
1 piece 7 inches
1 piece 6 inches

**2** Wrap a 33-inch piece of chain around your arm to make your armhole and secure it with a jump ring. *If you need to make the 33-inch pieces longer, now is the time to add the extra length you want.*

**3** Repeat for the other arm.

**4** Take the 10-inch chain and, on every other link, add a jump ring with a safety pin hanging from it. This is going to take a while, so pop in your favorite DVD and hunker down.

**5** Repeat step 4 for all of the remaining pieces of chain (except the armhole chains!).

**6** Add crystal beads on every few safety pins when you've completed your safety pin chains.

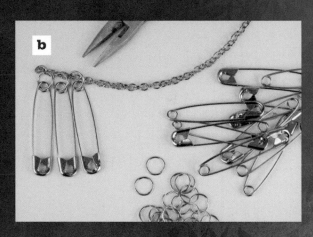

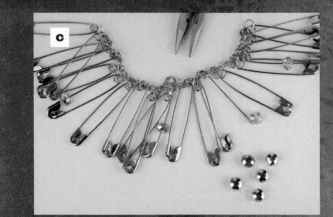

**7** Put on your armhole chains and measure where you would like your first layer of safety pins to lie. Secure the piece across your chest with a jump ring. You could get some help from a friend, or mark it with a pin and use the exact measurement on the other side.

**8** Repeat step 7 on the other, making sure that the chains are spaced symmetrically on both sides. Work from the largest safety pin chain to the smallest.

# BOBBY PIN FRINGE

I challenged myself to do something a bit different with bobby pins for this book, and it was tough. Most of what I came up with initially had an Egyptian look, and I had a sneaking suspicion it had been done before. I thought this was a nice take on bobby pin jewelry. Using different colored pins for this might be really fun. Just a thought.

## YOU'LL NEED

- 25 inches of large-link silver-tone chain (look for chain that a bobby pin will fit over easily—not too thick—and links that will take 5 bobby pins)
- Needle-nose pliers (and wirecutters if the pliers don't have them)
- 125 bobby pins
- 2 silver-tone jump rings
- 1 silver-tone lobster claw closure

## HERE'S HOW

**1** Cut your chain into two pieces, 16 inches and 9 inches long.

**2** Starting in the center of the 16-inch piece, push five bobby pins through each link, working your way up symmetrically on both sides from the middle of the chain. Continue until you've put five bobby pins on 14 links.

**3** Fill 11 links on the 9-inch chain, again starting in the middle and working your way up.

**4** Take the end links of the shorter chain and attach them to the longer chain where the bobby pins end on both sides. Leave a couple of links in between the last set of bobby pins and the end link.

**5** Add jump rings to the ends of the longer chain and a lobster claw on one side for the closure.

# FEATHER FANTASTIC!

I have used feathers in my design work forever, and I'm not entirely sure, but I think this might be my favorite use of a feather design to date. How great would this look on a handbag!

*Suggestion:*
Try mixing silver feathers with gold feathers.

## YOU'LL NEED

- Jacket
- 66 large safety pins per feather (nos. 3 or 4)
- 28 (1½-inch) safety pins per feather
- 22 inches of crystal chain per feather
- Needle-nose pliers (and wirecutters if the pliers don't have them)
- E-6000 glue

## HERE'S HOW

**1** Decide where you want your feathers on your jacket.

**2** Cut 22 inches of crystal chain per feather. Lay your jacket flat and glue the crystal chain to the jacket with a thin line of E-6000 glue and let dry. This is your feather's spine. Give it some gentle curves.

**3** Starting with your larger safety pins and leaving about 5 inches at the base of your spine, create the feather by pinning up one side and angling them more and more acutely until you reach the top of the spine. The top safety pin of the feather is aligned with the direction of the spine at the top.

**4** At the base of the feather, create "fluff" by fixing the pins in a more random order, but making sure they are still pinned in the same general direction, as shown in photo d. These pins are not placed as uniformly as the larger pins.

*Hint:*
This is definitely a hand-wash, dry-clean, or spot-clean item.

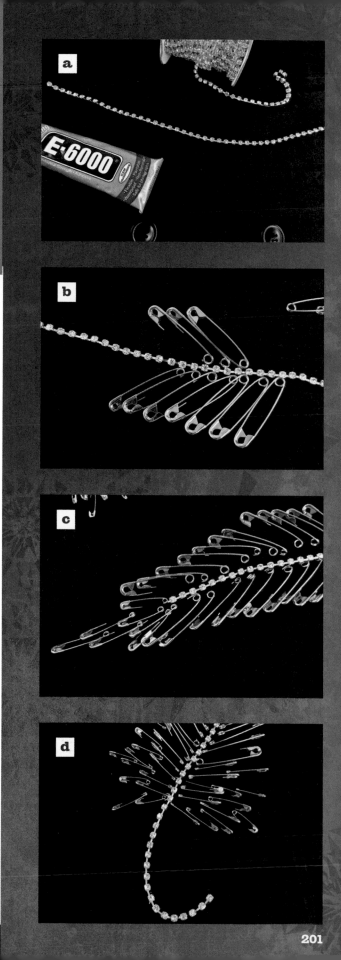

# BOBBY'S RED GEM NECKLACE AND EARRINGS

I wanted to do something different with bobby pins—something that hadn't been seen before—and this is what I came up with. I think we need to further explore how we can make these affordable little wires into amazing pieces of jewelry. I'm sure you can come up with some piece of your own . . . and when you do, make sure to let me know, okay?

## YoU'LL NeeD

### FOR THE NECKLACE

- 45 bobby pins
- 18 flat-back crystal or acrylic gems (1-inch diameter)
- E-6000 glue
- 11 gunmetal jump rings
- 16 inches of black chain (www.createforless.com)
- 1 lobster claw closure
- Needle-nose pliers (and wirecutters if the pliers don't have them)

### FOR THE EARRINGS

- 2 gunmetal earring wires

## HeRE's HoW

**1** Glue five bobby pins to the back of one of your gems with E-6000, making sure that the middle bobby pin extends above the edge of the gem. This is where you will attach a jump ring and hang it from the chain.

**2** Add some E-6000 to another gem. Sandwich the five bobby pins between the two gems and let dry.

**3** Make nine of these (but if you're making the matching earrings, make two more).

4  Attach a jump ring to the bobby pin that is sticking out from the gems and attach it to your black chain at the exact center.

5  Continue adding your bobby pin gems to your necklace, working your way out evenly from the center.

6  Add jump rings to the ends of the chain and a lobster claw for the closure.

## FOR THE EARRINGS

1  Make two bobby pin gems following the instructions for the necklace.

2  Add a jump ring and an earring wire to make your earrings.

Now, that was easy, wasn't it?

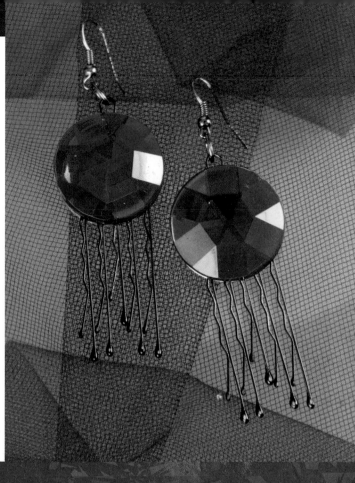

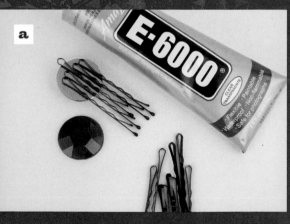

# PIN AND PEARLS

Why not inject a little glamour into something traditionally associated with punk? Add some pearls to pins and a few crystals and faster than you can say "mosh pit," you've got an amazing statement piece that is sure to put you center stage. Besides, it's safer to be center stage when people are moshing—that way, you won't ruin your dress.

## YOU'LL NEED

- 16 inches of large-link silver-tone chain
- 10 silver-tone chains of various sizes and lengths
- Needle-nose pliers (and wirecutters if the pliers don't have them)
- 60 large pearl beads
- 20 silver beads of various sizes
- 30 large (no. 3) safety pins
- 15 smaller safety pins in various sizes
- 30 silver-tone jump rings
- 3 large crystal or acrylic stitch-on gems

*Hint:*
Your necklace will likely look a bit different from mine . . . But, knowing you, it will turn out *much, much* better!

# HeRE's HoW

**1** Cut a 16-inch piece of large chain. This is your base chain from which everything will hang.

**2** Take 15 large safety pins, string them with pearls, and close them.

**3** Add a jump ring to each end of the pin and attach one to a 6-inch piece of chain and the other to the base chain about 6 inches from the end.

**4** Add another jump ring to the end of the base chain and attach it asymmetrically a few inches away so that it hangs from the base chain.

**5** Cut small pieces of chain anywhere from 2 inches to 3 inches in length and attach them with the safety pins. This will add heft and a more jumbled look to your piece.

**6** Continue with small pieces of chain anywhere from 3 inches to 6 inches in length, hanging them from both the base chain and the other chains.

**7** Hang pins without chains from jump rings throughout to fill up blank spaces.

**8** When your necklace is filled with chains, pearls, and pins, decide where you are going to hang your crystals and attach them with jump rings.

**9** Use another large safety pin as a closure in the back by pinning it through the last links in your chain.

# BOBBY PIN COUTURE

I can see this piece walking down a runway in Milan during Fashion Week, sending everyone scrambling to get their hands on it. Can't you see it with a Prada dress and a big square handbag?

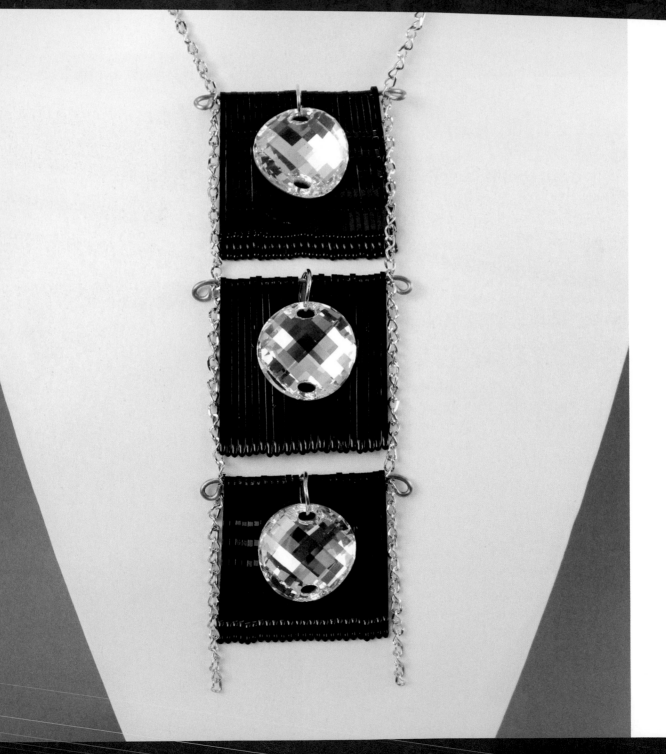

## YOU'LL NEED

- 9 inches of heavy-gauge wire that doesn't bend easily
- Needle-nose pliers (and wirecutters if the pliers don't have them)
- 36 inches of medium silver-tone chain
- 75 bobby pins
- 3 large stitch-on crystals or acrylic gems
- 5 large silver-tone jump rings
- 1 silver-tone lobster claw closure

## HERE's HOW

1. Cut your wire into three equal pieces and bend loops on one side of each piece with your needle-nose pliers.

2. Cut two 18-inch pieces of chain. Thread the wire through one of the chains about 2½ inches from the end.

3. String 25 bobby pins along the wire and thread the wire through the other chain the same distance from the end.

4. Create another loop with your needle-nose pliers. This will keep it in place.

5. Working your way up the chains, measure above the first set of bobby pins the length of a bobby pin plus ⅜ inch and thread your second wire through the chains.

6. Repeat steps 3 and 4.

7. Repeat steps 3, 4, and 5 for the last row of bobby pins.

8. Add jump rings to the end of your chains and a lobster claw for the closure.

9. Hang the crystals from jump rings at the center of each row of bobby pins.

# HaTs OfF to YoU!

atpins used to be part of everyone's daily attire. Now we rarely see them. I decided that it was time to bring them back—even if you don't wear a hat! These would look amazing pinned on the lapel of a jacket or on the flap of a handbag. One way or another, I'm going to make sure that the PIN is IN!

# BIRD HATPIN

I've worn this hat to a fashion show and *wow*, did people go nuts. Perhaps it was a little teensy-weensy bit flamboyant for a guy to wear, but who cares. I had a blast wearing it! It was even more fun making it. I'm hoping that feathers stay in style for a long time to come. I know that they always look terrific on hats.

## Hint:

Many of these items can be purchased at www.createforless.com!

## YOU'LL NEED

- Melt Art Mold-n-Pour molding putty
- Plastic bird figurine
- ICE Resin or Smooth-Cast 300
- Lumiere Halo Blue Gold metallic paint (see Resource Guide)
- Paintbrush
- Hatpin blank (find one at www.buy.com)
- Feather hackle pad (a finished group of several feathers attached to fabric), about 5 inches by 7 inches
- E-6000 glue
- Rubber or plastic gloves

## HeRE's HoW

1 Knead the molding putty according to the instructions that I provide on page 232 and spread it around the bird head figurine. (If you need to, review the Mold & Cast, Bold and

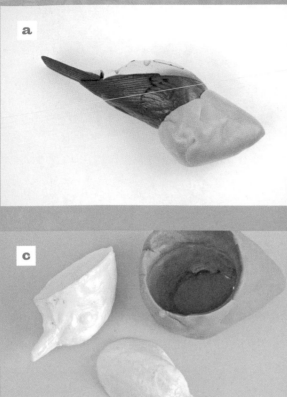

Fast! chapter.) Your mold will be done in 10 minutes!

2  Mix your resin (outside and wearing gloves) or mix your Smooth-Cast 300 casting liquid. Fill your bird mold as shown in photo b and let set.

3  Remove the cast bird head after it's set, paint it with the Lumiere Halo Blue Gold, and let dry.

4  Stick the blunt end of the hatpin through the back of the feather hackle pad so that it sticks out on top, just under where your bird head will be. You will have to work it through the fabric.

5  Using a generous amount of E-6000, glue your bird head on top of the feather hackle pad while sandwiching the hatpin in between and let dry.

# VINTAGE IMAGE HATPIN

I say we bring back the hatpin! It's been neglected far too long. I, for one, am a huge
fan of hats, since my hair has a mind of its own. When that happens, I silence it with
a chic chapeau! After I finished this project, I thought of how much cooler it would
have been with a photo of my grandpa! You can use whatever image you want for this
project. Make several and wear them at the same time!

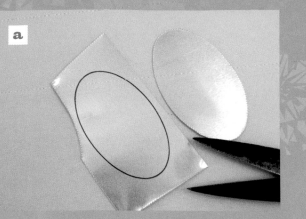

## You'll Need

- Aluminum flashing
- Tin shears or heavy-duty scissors with serrated blades
- Scrap wood
- Image you want to use (see page 374)
- Scissors
- Elmer's Glue-All
- E-6000 glue
- Small piece of leather or vinyl
- ICE Resin or Mod Podge Dimensional Magic
- Hatpin blank (see Resource Guide)

## Here's How

1. Cut your aluminum flashing into an oval the size you want for the top of the hatpin with tin shears or heavy-duty serrated scissors.

2. Cut out your image so that it's just a bit smaller than the aluminum oval shape.

3. In the leather or vinyl, cut out an oval just a bit smaller than your aluminum oval.

4. Carefully glue the image on the aluminum oval with Elmer's Glue-All and let dry.

5. Coat your image with ICE Resin (see page 232 for tips and instructions for use) or Mod Podge Dimensional Magic and let dry.

6. Glue your hatpin on the back with E-6000 and then glue the vinyl or leather oval as a backing and let dry.

# RINGS AND FEATHERS HATPIN

I've been hitting the dollar store for kooky rings to use on other projects. Mainly hatpins. It seems like the less I want to comb my hair, the more I want to wear a cool hat so people won't know how truly lazy I am in the morning. There are tons of rings to choose from, and they are all perfect for this project. Because the rings are inexpensive, they are really easy to take apart. BTW, I think this pin would look terrific on a blazer, too.

## YOU'LL NEED

- Ring you can take apart
- Wirecutters
- Iron and ironing board (or a countertop with a towel, which is what I use)
- 12 inches of 2-inch ribbon or fabric that you can iron into a 2-inch band
- Hot glue gun and glue sticks
- E-6000 glue
- Hatpin blank (see Resource Guide)
- Goose feathers in colors you like (www.createforless.com has a terrific selection)

## HERE'S HOW

1. Cut an 8-inch piece of ribbon or fabric strip and fold in the ends so they meet in the center. Glue the ends down in the center with tiny dabs of hot glue.

2. Pinch the bow in the center and hot-glue it in place.

3. Take your 4-inch piece of ribbon and fold in the ends horizontally so that it's only ¾ inch wide and press.

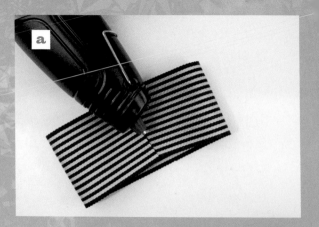

**4** Wrap the ¾-inch piece around the center of your folded 8-inch piece twice and hot-glue the ends down in the back to create a bow. To make it neater in the back, you might want to tuck down the edge of the folded ribbon piece so it has a finished edge.

**5** With wirecutters, remove the decorative piece on your ring. It should come off easily.

**6** Take five or six goose feathers and hot glue them to the back of your decorative ring component.

**7** Glue the ring component with feathers using E-6000 to the front of the bow and let dry. Be neat; you don't want to see the glue.

**8** Wriggle the blunt end of your hatpin inside the back of the bow and glue in place with a generous dab of E-6000 and let dry.

# SCRAPPY FLOWER HATPIN

This is a simple gift to make someone who likes to wear hats. You could also wear it on a blazer or without the long pin—it could make a supercool brooch. I used a few little scraps of leather and vinyl that I just couldn't throw away. Hey, you never know when you'll need something again, right?

## YOU'LL NEED

- Piece of brown leather or suede 8 inches by 4 inches
- 1 piece of green leather or suede 8 inches by 4 inches
- 1 piece of beige leather or suede 3 inches by 3 inches
- 1 piece of green vinyl, leather, or suede 4 inches by 4 inches
- 4 inches of brown leather cord
- 1 pearl
- E-6000 glue
- Hot glue gun and glue sticks
- Hatpin blank (see Resource Guide)

*Hint:*
www.createforless.com
has all the colors
of cord!

## HeRE's HoW

1. Using the large flower pattern on page 367, cut out a large brown flower and two green flowers just a tiny bit smaller than the brown.

2. Using the smaller flower pattern, cut out a brown flower and then a beige flower that is just a tiny bit smaller than the brown one.

3. Roll your strip of cord like a cinnamon roll and hot glue the end down so it makes a disk.

4. With E-6000, glue your hatpin to the large brown flower.

5. Glue the large green flower on top of that.

6. Glue on the next brown flower and then glue the beige flower on top of that.

7. Glue down your disk and then add the pearl in the center.

8. Flip over your hatpin and add the second green flower on the back.

I like using doll heads in my work. Not sure why, I just do. I get that some of you out there find them creepy, and that's okay. I feel the same way about clowns. If you've been following my work these past twelve years, you know that I like to use doll heads from time to time. Joseph Cornell and many other influential artists loved using them, too, so I feel I'm in good company. If doll faces just are not for you, try replacing them with something else! How about a lion head or bird head? These projects are sure to look just as interesting with your favorite objects.

# BABY HEAD NECKLACE

I feel sometimes that doll heads have a soul or that they are staring back at me. If you're not a fan, use something else, like a bird or a flower. Whatever you do, don't make a mold of a clown! That would push me over the edge.

## YOU'LL NEED

- Melt Art Mold-n-Pour molding putty (www.createforless.com)
- Baby head or 3-D object you want to mold
- ICE Resin or Smooth-Cast 300
- Drill with small drill bit
- Lumiere metallic blue paint
- Medium silver-tone chain in length you want
- 3 large silver-tone jump rings
- 1 silver-tone lobster claw closure
- Needle-nose pliers (and wirecutters if the pliers don't have them)

## HeRE's HoW

**1** Knead your two-part molding putty according to instructions that I provide on page 232. (If you need to, review the Mold & Cast, Bold and Fast! chapter.) It's supereasy, and once you get started, you'll be addicted to it like I am! Smoosh it over the doll face, making sure that you have a decent amount around the face and that it's covering all the parts you want to cast.

**2** Let the mold set for 10 minutes. Yes, that's all it takes! Remove your new mold.

**3** Mix your resin (outside and wearing gloves) or mix your Smooth-Cast 300 casting liquid. Fill your mold and let set.

4 Remove cast head from the mold and drill a small hole at the top.

5 Paint your entire piece with the Lumiere blue metallic paint and let dry.

6 Cut the length of chain you want and hang the piece from a jump ring at the center of the chain.

7 Add jump rings to the ends of the chain and a lobster claw for the closure.

# CRYSTAL PUNK BABY HEAD

What can I say? It happened late one night and I'm not apologizing for it. It's crazy, kooky, and weird . . . and I LOVE IT!

# YOU'LL NEED

- Melt Art Mold-n-Pour molding putty (www.createforless.com)
- Doll head or 3-D object you want to mold
- ICE Resin or Smooth-Cast 300
- Krylon Flat black spray paint
- Large black crystal—choice of size and shape up to you
- Enough crystal chain to circle the baby head and crystal
- Crystal beads
- 16 inches large silver-tone chain
- 4 large silver-tone jump rings
- 25 safety pins of various sizes (8 of them large no. 3 size)
- Plastic gutter guard
- Scissors
- Aluminum flashing
- Tin shears or heavy-duty scissors with serrated blades
- E-6000 glue
- Needle-nose pliers (and wirecutters if the pliers don't have them)

# HeRE's How

**1** Knead your two-part molding putty according to the instructions that I provide on page 232. (If you need to, review the Mold & Cast, Bold and Fast! chapter.) It's supereasy, and once you get started, you'll be addicted to it like I am! Smoosh it over the doll face, making sure that there is a decent amount around the face and that it's covering all the parts you want to cast.

**2** Let the mold set for 10 minutes. Yes, that's all it takes! Remove your new mold.

**3** Mix your resin (outside and wearing gloves) or mix your Smooth-Cast 300 casting liquid (this can be done inside). Fill your mold and let set.

**4** Remove the doll head, spray paint with the Krylon flat black, and let dry.

**5** With tin shears or heavy-duty scissors with serrated blades, cut an oval a little under 3 inches by 4 inches from the aluminum flashing and glue your head to the oval with E-6000.

**6** Glue the large black crystal to the top of the head.

**7** With dabs of E-6000 on a toothpick, surround the head and crystal with crystal chain and let dry.

**8** Glue the entire piece to a larger oval cut from gutter guard.

**9** Add six crystal beads to two of the large safety pins and then add them to the upper part of the gutter guard with two jump rings.

**10** Cut two 8-inch pieces of silver-tone chain and add them to the other ends of the safety pins.

**10** Hang the other safety pins from the bottom of the gutter guard. Hang the smaller pins from the sides and the large pins from the bottom.

**12** Add crystals to the larger pins for some more sparkle. Close your necklace with another large safety pin.

# BABY CLUTCH

I'm sure right now you're wondering what actually goes through my head to inspire something like this. Not sure, really. What I can tell you is that I'm not the first, nor will I be the last, to use doll imagery in my work. I was recently at the Metropolitan Museum of Art in New York City and saw some amazing moody black-and-white photographs from the early 1920s that featured broken dolls sitting on swings and in alleyways. That was freaky! This, well, it's just a funky wallet to get the attention of all who witness you pulling it out of your purse. Come on, it's not like I put a clown on it!

## YOU'LL NEED

- Wallet in need of a makeover
- Cast of a doll head (see page 220 for casting instructions and materials)
- E-6000 glue
- Lumiere metallic paint in Pearl Turquoise and Pewter
- Paintbrush
- Rags
- Masking tape
- 12 inches of crystal chain
- Needle-nose pliers (and wirecutters if the pliers don't have them)
- 1 black cord tassel (www.createforless.com)
- Krylon Glitter Blast in Starry Night
- Minwax Clear Aerosol Lacquer
- Krylon gray primer
- Toothpicks

## HERE'S HOW

**1** Make a mold and cast a doll face that you like. (See instructions and materials on page 232. It's easy and fun!)

**2** Paint the doll face in the Lumiere Pearl Turquoise and let dry.

**3** With a rag, rub the pewter paint over the doll face to give it sheen and definition.

**4** Mask off the zipper on your clutch with tape. Spray the clutch on both sides with gray primer and let dry.

**5** Spray the clutch with the Glitter Blast on each side and let dry.

**6** Spray the clutch with Minwax Clear Aerosol Lacquer and let dry. This will eliminate any tackiness in your spray-painted projects and give them an amazing finish. (This is the best-kept secret about eliminating tackiness from spray-painted objects.)

**7** Center your doll face on the clutch and glue it on with E-6000.

**8** Cut 12 inches of crystal chain. With dabs of E-6000 on a toothpick, carefully add the crystal chain around the doll face.

**9** Remove the old zipper or zipper pull and hang the black tassel from it.

# HOT PINK DOLL FACE CUFF

You're either Team Doll Head or you're not. I am the captain, president, chairman, and CEO of Team Doll Head. Membership requirements are simple . . . you must love doll heads, doll parts, doll faces and stuff made with doll heads. Oh, and send me a check for $50, please—your certificate of membership will be in the mail upon receipt.

## YOU'LL NEED

- Melt Art Mold-n-Pour molding putty (www.createforless.com)
- Doll head or 3-D object you want to mold
- ICE Resin or Smooth-Cast 300
- Plastic gutter guard
- Aluminum flashing
- Tin shears or heavy-duty scissors with serrated blades
- Scrap wood
- E-6000 glue
- Pink fluorescent Krylon spray paint
- Lumiere metallic paint in pewter
- Rags
- Enough crystal chain to surround your doll face
- Large crystal button (your choice)
- 1 rubber hairband
- 3 inches of 20-gauge wire
- Needle-nose pliers (and wirecutters if the pliers don't have them)

## HERE'S HOW

**1** Knead your two-part molding putty according to instructions that I provide on page 232. (If you need to, review the Mold & Cast, Bold and Fast! chapter.) It's supereasy, and once you get started, you'll be addicted to it like I am! Smoosh it over the doll face, making sure that you have a decent amount around the

face and that it's covering all the parts you want to cast. Let the mold set for 10 minutes. Yes, that's all it takes! Remove your new mold.

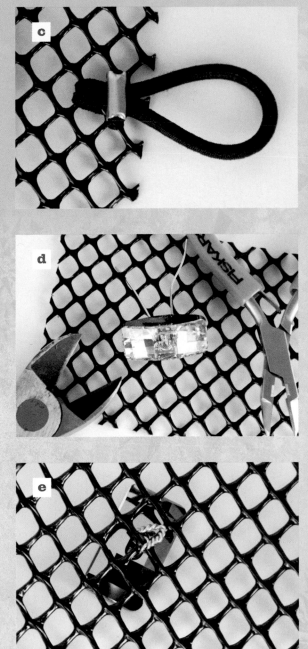

2 Mix your resin (outside and wearing gloves) or mix your Smooth-Cast 300 casting liquid. Fill your mold and let set.

3 Remove your doll face from the mold, spray-paint it fluorescent pink, and let dry.

4 Paint your doll face with the Jacquard Lumiere pewter and immediately wipe off the paint so that it leaves details and some shimmer on the pink doll face.

5 Cut a piece of gutter guard 3 inches by 9 inches with heavy-duty scissors.

6 Cut a piece of aluminum flashing a bit larger than the doll face and glue the doll face to the aluminum flashing with E-6000 and let dry.

7 Trim the aluminum flashing around the doll face leaving about ¼ inch all the way around.

8 With dabs of E-6000 on a toothpick, carefully glue the crystal chain around the doll face on the flashing and let dry.

9 Glue the face to the center of your gutter guard piece and let dry.

10 Secure your button to the end of the gutter guard cuff with wire. Twist it in place, bend so that it's not sharp, and cut off excess.

12 Measure how big you need your cuff and secure your rubber hairband with a slip knot around the other end of the cuff, then stretch the hairband over the button for the closure.

# PEARLY DOLL FACE

Admit it, you love it when people notice you and comment on your signature style! We all do. Wearing this cuff will be sure to get you noticed. Okay, maybe not always the way you planned, but at least it will be a conversation starter, right?

## YOU'LL NEED

- Melt Art Mold-n-Pour molding putty (www.createforless.com)
- Baby head or 3-D object you want to mold
- ICE Resin or Smooth-Cast 300
- Lumiere metallic paint in Pewter
- Paintbrush
- Metal cuff

- Krylon Fusion for Plastic in flat black
- Rags
- Aluminum flashing
- Tin shears or heavy-duty scissors with serrated blades
- Scrap wood
- E-6000 glue
- Toothpicks
- Selection of pearls, flat-back gems, and crystal beads

## HeRE's How

**1** Knead your two-part molding putty according to instructions that I provide on page 232. (If you need to, review the Mold & Cast, Bold and Fast! chapter.) Smoosh it over the doll face, making sure that you have a decent amount around the face and it's covering all the parts you want to cast.

**2** Let the mold set for 10 minutes. Remove your new mold. Mix your resin (outside and wearing gloves) or mix your Smooth-Cast 300 casting liquid. Fill your mold and let set.

**3** Remove your doll head from the mold, paint it with the Lumiere pewter, and let dry.

**4** Spray-paint your cuff with flat black Krylon Fusion for Plastic.

**5** Spray the cuff lightly with the pewter paint and then rub with a rag, to give it some shimmer.

**6** Cut an oval 3 inches by 4 inches out of your aluminum flashing with tin shears or heavy-duty serrated scissors.

**7** Glue the doll face to the oval with E-6000.

**8** Glue the oval to the cuff with E-6000 and let dry.

**9** With dabs of E-6000 on a toothpick, carefully glue gems and pearls around the doll face.

**10** Add more pearls and stones under the oval and on the sides of the cuff until you're satisfied with the design.

# MoLd & CaST, bOLD AND FaSt!

If you look around your house (or your grandmother's house), I'm sure you can find something from which to make a mold. I've used refrigerator magnets, plastic birds, twigs, and bold pieces of jewelry. Use your imagination and go nuts. Once you've made your molds, you have some options as to what to use to cast your shapes. If you are impatient and want to get going quickly, try the Smooth-Cast 300 (www.smooth-on.com). This is a two-part liquid plastic mix that sets in about 10 minutes and you're ready to start almost immediately. Mix two equal parts of the Smooth-Cast 300 and pour it directly into your mold and in about 10 minutes it's hard. It doesn't have harsh fumes, so you're able to use it inside. Smooth-on makes a variety of different products, but the Smooth-Cast 300 is what you'll want to use when ordering from them. If you have a little more patience and want your cast pieces to be clear as ICE, then ICE Resin is my favorite casting system (see page 232). ICE Resin is a jeweler-quality resin that dries hard as a rock. ICE Resin has fumes that can give you a headache if you don't follow the instructions and work outside or in a VERY well-ventilated area. You'll also need to let the pieces dry in a room or part of the house that you don't use. For both Smooth-on and ICE Resin you're better off wearing rubber or plastic gloves to keep the components off your hands. They are sticky! The pieces on these next few pages use some of my favorite molds. Use your imagination and you won't be disappointed, I promise.

# MOLD MAKING AND CASTING IN LESS THAN ONE HOUR!

I always thought casting was just too complicated, but I was wrong. With just a few simple products, I've been able to make amazing things in less than an hour! You heard me, LESS THAN ONE HOUR! It's amazing what modern science has developed for us crafters, and rubber molds are no exception. Thanks to the folks at Ranger, you can make a mold in 10 minutes. I found a company called Smooth-On that makes a two-part liquid plastic that sets in just 10 to 15 minutes. If you're impatient like I am, these products are the answer to your casting and mold-making dreams.

## PrODUcTs I rEcOmMeNd

### MELT ART MOLD-N-POUR BY RANGER

(www.createforless.com)

This is a two-part putty that you mix together and smooth over an object. After letting it set for 10 minutes, you can remove a ready-to-use rubber mold. You have to work pretty quickly because once it sets, it's set for good. I've had wonderful results almost every time with this product, and you can use it on almost anything.

### SMOOTH-CAST 300 SERIES BRIGHT WHITE LIQUID PLASTIC

Smooth-On sells many casting kits (rubber, silicone, resins), but the Smooth-Cast 300 is a two-part liquid plastic that you mix together and pour into your molds and it's what I recommend for the projects I've created. It sets in 10 minutes, and in about 15 minutes you can start painting it. This stuff is A-M-A-Z-I-N-G and you can use it inside because there are virtually no fumes, unlike resin products. And it's my little secret! They also sell a two-part putty that works just as well as the Melt Art Mold-n-Pour.

### ICE RESIN

(www.iceresin.com)

ICE is a two-part resin that creates jeweler-quality cast pieces. I've also discovered that by painting on the resin with a disposable brush, you can harden things like lace and fabric and coat cardboard so that they're hard as a rock! Just mix your ICE Resin with your disposable brush, paint it on your lace or cardboard, making sure that all of the areas are covered, and let it dry on wax paper. ICE Resin sets overnight and creates beautiful, clear pieces that do not yellow over time, and I find it to be the best two-part resin on the market. If you're patient and willing to give it the proper amount of drying time, it's worth using this product. I always recommend mixing it outdoors and letting it set in a room that you're not sleeping or working in. Just follow the instructions carefully and make sure to mix the equal parts thoroughly. Work on wax paper because the resin won't stick to it, and always wear rubber or plastic gloves so that you don't get sticky hands. Also, it dries faster if you leave it under a desk lamp undisturbed. Not much faster, but you can shave off a few hours of your time.

# TWO-TONE GLITTER BLAST HANDBAG

If you ever hit a sale on cheap handbags or find one at a thrift shop that has a good shape, just grab it and add some sparkle to it. There is nothing more fun than having something that NO ONE else has. It's even more fun when you tell them that you made it yourself. These bags were a bargain at just three bucks each. With a little bit of Krylon Glitter Blast, you'll be ready for the runway.

## YoU'LL NeED

- Handbag in need of remodeling
- Mold and cast of a piece of jewelry that you like (see page 232)
- Lumiere metallic paints in Pewter and Old Brass
- Piece of vinyl or leather
- Fiskars pinking shears
- Base color of paint to match the Glitter Blast*
- Krylon Glitter Blast in two colors
- Newspaper
- Masking tape
- Minwax Clear Aerosol Lacquer
- E-6000 glue

*I used metallic gold for the gold purse and gray for the silver purse

## HeRE's HoW

1. Figure out what kind of centerpiece you want for your bag and make your mold and cast. (See instructions and materials for molding and casting on page 232.)

2. Paint your cast piece to match the colors of your handbag.

3. Cut out an oval from your vinyl or leather big enough for you to mount your cast piece. I used pinking shears for the edges.

4. Spray-paint your entire bag and centerpiece oval in a base color that matches the color of your Glitter Blast. I used gold for the gold bag and gray for the silver bag.

5. When the base is dry, cover the sections using newspaper and masking tape and spray your first section of Glitter Blast.

6. Flip over and repeat.

7. Remove the taped-off section and tape off again for your second color, then add your second color of Glitter Blast.

8. Here's the best-kept secret about keeping spray-painted objects from getting tacky: After spray-painting, spray with Minwax Clear Aerosol Lacquer and let dry. This will eliminate any tackiness in your spray-painted projects, as well as give an amazing finish and keep your glitter intact.

9. With E-6000, glue on your oval, but not the molded piece yet. Put something flat and heavy like a book on top so it dries evenly.

10. Glue your molded piece on the oval with E-6000 and let dry.

# I AIN'T LION

My friend Shaye (I've written about her before) will automatically think this belongs to her because she's a Leo. She's also a jewelry hoarder. Suffice it to say, it will be making its way to her jewelry box after I photograph it for this book.

*Hint:*
You don't have to make a casting for this; you could just use a brooch and tons of matching chain. I like creating molds and casts because then I'm positive that no one else has a piece like this!

## YOU'LL NEED

- Cast of lion or anything you want (see page 232) (or you could use a brooch for this project)
- Krylon spray adhesive
- Gold leaf
- 1-inch flat brush
- Pin back
- E-6000 glue
- 3 yards of fine gold-tone chain
- Needle-nose pliers (and wirecutters if the pliers don't have them)
- 2 gold-tone jump rings
- 1 gold-tone lobster claw closure

## HERE'S HOW

**1** Make your lion mold and cast (or any cast you want to use for this), or find a suitable brooch. It's up to you. I used a lion head kitchen magnet for this project. (See instructions and materials for molding and casting on page 232.) Spray your cast piece or brooch with Krylon adhesive. Brush on gold leaf and let dry.

**2** Glue on your pin back with E-6000 and let dry.

**3** Cut two 8-inch and two 10-inch pieces of chain.

**4** Open your pin back and loop one 10-inch chain and one 8-inch chain onto the pin.

**5** With the rest of the chain, create fringe on the pin, threading the pin through the links until the pin is almost filled up.

**6** Finish by adding the second 8-inch piece of chain and then the second 10-inch piece of chain. Close the pin.

**7** Add jump rings to the ends of both sets of chains and a lobster claw for the closure.

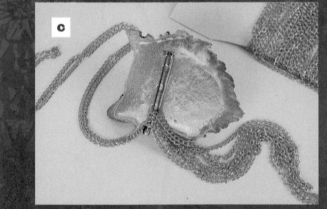

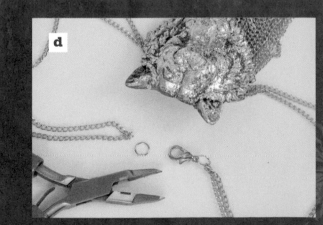

# I AIN'T LION CAST SHOE CLIPS

This project is really about using a cast piece to create a beautiful shoe clip. It can be done with any cast piece that you want, but I found this lion fridge magnet and couldn't resist casting it into an amazing shoe clip. Grab any unusual objects like faces on sculptures or interesting pieces of jewelry to do the same. Just follow the instructions on page 232 for making molds and casting, and you're halfway there!

## YOU'LL NEED

- 2 cast pieces in a shape that you like
- Spray adhesive
- Gold leaf
- Flat paintbrush
- Minwax Polycrylic clear coat
- 2 clip-on earring blanks
- E-6000 glue

## HERE'S HOW

1. Mold and cast two shapes that you like. (See instructions and materials for molding and casting on page 232.)
2. Spray with the spray adhesive.
3. Carefully add your gold leaf with a paintbrush and let dry.
4. Coat your lion with Minwax Polycrylic clear coat and let dry.
5. Using a generous amount of E-6000, glue your earring back on to the upper part of the shape and let dry. Be sure to glue the curved part of the earring back, not the flat disk area.

# SONG BIRDS

Hit any thrift or dollar store, and you'll find a ceramic bird perfect for mold-making and ideal for this necklace. You could even use five different objects for something like this. The key with *this* piece is repetition. Repetition. Repetition.

## YOU'LL NEED

- Mold of bird head (see page 232)
- Aluminum flashing
- Tin shears or heavy-duty shears with serrated edge blades
- Hammer and sharp nail
- Scrap wood
- Lumiere metallic paint in a color you like (I used Halo Blue)
- Paintbrush
- E-6000 glue
- 16 inches of silver-tone chain (or longer if you need)
- 7 silver-tone jump rings
- 1 lobster claw closure

## HERE'S HOW

1. Cast five of your birds (See instructions and materials for molding and casting on page 232.). This might take a while if you're using ICE Resin, which needs to set overnight. I might consider using the Smooth-Cast 300 for something with more than one cast piece.

2. Cut a piece of aluminum flashing 4 inches by 6 inches. Trace the base of each piece on the aluminum flashing and cut out a bit bigger all the way around.

3. On a piece of scrap wood to protect your work surface, tap a hole with your hammer and sharp nail at the top of each oval shape where you will be hanging your bird. I put a dot on the tin where I wanted my holes.

**4** Flip each aluminum piece over and tap the hole to eliminate sharp edges.

**5** Paint each piece with several coats of the Jacquard Lumiere metallic paint and let dry.

**6** Glue the birds to the ovals with E-6000, making sure not to cover the holes.

**7** When the glue is dry, add a jump ring to each bird and place your first bird in the exact center of the chain.

**8** Measure how far apart you want each bird and add them to the chain evenly all the way around.

**9** Add jump rings to the ends of the chain and a lobster claw for the closure.

# TAKE A BOW

There is a scene in the movie *Auntie Mame* with Rosalind Russell that has always stuck with me: As she's about to head out to Christmas dinner with her future husband (though she doesn't know it), she grabs a piece of mistletoe from the tree and plops it on her hat. And it looks amazing. She then does the same for her maid. I've never forgotten how something that simple could be so dramatic. It's why I love making fabric bows for clothing. You can do it in a heartbeat and it always adds that extra something. I put this one on the waist of a bias-cut draped plaid dress and it looks wonderful.

## YOU'LL NEED

- Cast of face or a brooch (see page 232)
- ½ yard of fabric
- ¼ yard of a matching taffeta
- Scissors
- Fiskars pinking shears
- Needle and thread
- Hot glue gun and glue sticks
- Pin back

*Hint:*

"Cutting on the bias" is when you cut diagonally instead of straight up and down on the fabric. You can do this by folding your ½ yard in a triangle, matching up the edges, and then cutting along that diagonal line.

## HERE'S HOW

**1** Figure out what kind of centerpiece you want. You can use an existing piece, or make your mold and cast. (See instructions and materials for molding and casting on page 232.)

**2** Cut your first ½ yard of fabric on the bias in 2-inch strips. You will need about 4 feet of 2-inch bias.

**3** Cut your matching ¼ yard taffeta fabric in ½-inch strips using pinking shears.

**4** Fold your fabric bias strips into a bow about 6 inches across and stitch together in the center.

**5** Fold your ½-inch pinked strips into a bow about 6 inches wide and stitch to the fabric bow in the center.

**6** Cut the loops on the pinked fabric bow.

**7** Hot-glue your cast face or pin your brooch to the center of the bow.

**8** Hot-glue your pin back to the back of the bow (or stitch it, it's up to you).

# THORNS AND HUMMINGBIRDS

I have always been in love with Frida Kahlo's *Self-Portrait with Thorn Necklace and Hummingbird*. Recently I was able to view the actual painting in Los Angeles, and it blew me away. So, I thought it was time to create something inspired by this magnificent painting.

## YOU'LL NEED

- Cast of twig that you like (see page 232)
- Krylon
- ICE Resin or Smooth-Cast 300
- gray primer
- Lumiere metallic paint in Old Brass
- Paintbrush
- Copy of image on page 376
- Scissors
- Cardboard
- Elmer's Glue-All
- 2 yards of gold 18-gauge wire
- Needle-nose pliers (and wirecutters if the pliers don't have them)
- 12 gold-tone jump rings
- Large pin
- 14 inches of medium gold-tone chain
- 1 silver-tone lobster claw closure
- Rubber or plastic gloves

## HERE'S HOW

1. Create your twig mold and cast it at least six times. (See instructions and materials for molding and casting on page 232.) Since you need several casts of the twigs, you can do this step much more quickly if you use the Smooth-Cast 300 than with ICE Resin, since resin takes at least overnight to set.

2. Once your pieces are cast, spray them with the gray primer and let dry. Paint them with the Lumiere Old Brass and let dry.

3. Copy the bird image on page 376, glue it onto cardboard with Elmer's glue, and then carefully cut it out.

4. Mix your resin outside wearing gloves. Coat the bird and let dry overnight on wax paper in a room or area of the house that you don't use. If you don't want to mix ICE Resin for this step, you could use 3-D Crystal Lacquer to coat your bird.

5. Figure out how your twigs will go together.

6. Cut 10 to 12 pieces of wire about 6 inches long and wrap them around the ends of each twig by creating a loop at the end of the wires so they can be connected to another twig.

7. Once you've done this with your twigs, start linking the wires together with jump rings to hold your pattern.

8. Poke a hole with a large pin through the bird's beak (you may have to drill a small hole) and link it to the center of your twigs with a jump ring.

9. Cut two 7-inch pieces of chain. Add chains with jump rings to the end twigs. Add jump rings and a lobster claw for the closure.

## YoU'LL NeeD

- 2 Tyvec envelopes from the post office
- Scissors
- Sewing machine
- Lumiere metallic paints in several colors*
- Small paintbrushes
- E-6000 glue
- 20 different-size pearls
- Elmer's Glue-All
- Pin back

*I LOVE these paints, they make everything look amazing! See Resource Guide for some other Jacquard products and where to get them.

## HeRE's HoW

**1** Cut your Tyvec envclopes into as many 4-inch by 4-inch squares as you can.

**2** Layer three to four squares together and stitch through them with a freehand flower on your sewing machine. Don't worry about how perfect it is; the more *im*perfect, the better!

**3** Cut out the flower and make a 1-inch cut from between two petals to the center.

**4** Overlap just a small amount to make the flower dimensional (almost as if you're making a cone, but less severe).

**5** Stitch over it a few more times to help it keep the shape.

**6** Repeat steps 3 through 5 until you have four to five flowers cut in different sizes.

7 Paint the flowers with different colors of Lumiere metallic paint and let dry.

8 Glue the flowers together in the order you like with the E-6000 and let dry.

9 Glue the pearls in a cluster in the center of the flower with your Elmer's and let dry.

10 Add your pin to the back with the E-6000 and let dry.

# FUSING PLASTIC BAGS

It seems that everywhere I go, I get a plastic shopping bag, and honestly, they drive me nuts. There must be thousands of them under my sink. A friend told me about fusing them together with an iron and parchment paper, so I gave it a try—here's what I came up with. Though there weren't any noticeable fumes from my fusing projects, you still want to be safe and fuse outside or near an open window with some fresh air.

## SoME HiNtS
## FoR YoUr FUSiNG PRoJEcTs:

1. Don't worry if your bags get wrinkly or warped, that's part of the fun!

2. I like using four layers of bags for my fusing.

3. I keep the iron somewhere between notches 3 and 4 . . . but . . .

4. You'll have to experiment to make sure your iron isn't too hot and just melts the plastic.

5. Make sure all of your plastic is tucked between the parchment paper so you don't get melted plastic on your iron. Your mother will smack you for doing that!

# FUSED PLASTIC FLOWER CUFF

Why not make those plastic bags into something amazing and show the world they don't have to be so wasteful? This cuff is the perfect conversation piece as well as a great way to wow the world with your creativity!

## YOU'LL NEED

- Plastic bags
- Scissors (try Fiskars pinking shears for added texture)
- Iron and ironing board or countertop
- Parchment paper
- Needle and thread
- Lumiere metallic paints in several gold and bronze colors (see Resource Guide)
- Paintbrush
- Crystal beads or pearls, or a big gem
- E-6000 glue
- Velcro dots
- *Optional:* Sewing machine

## HeRE's HoW

1. Cut the handles and bottom off your plastic bags.

2. Stack four flat layers of plastic about the same size and sandwich them between two pieces of parchment paper.

3. Experiment with your iron to get the right setting (see page 255) and gently iron over the parchment paper. Your bags will shrink a little bit, but shouldn't melt. Check after every few swipes of the iron to see if the bags are fusing together. If they're not, you may need to turn the iron up a little bit.

4. Remove the fused plastic and cut out wavy circles or flower shapes.

5. To give your flowers dimension, put each flower between layers of parchment paper, touch down with the iron, and immediately remove them. This wrinkles them a little bit.

6. Cut out a rectangle about 8 inches by 2 inches (or the size you want for your cuff) from the fused plastic and stitch around it with needle and thread or on your sewing machine. I like to do this because it gives it more texture.

7. Paint the cuff and all the flower petals with the Lumiere metallic paints and let dry.

8. Stack your flower shapes from large to small.

9. With a needle and thread, stitch up from the bottom and add a bead. Continue with as many beads as you want for the center of the flower.

10. Glue on your cuff with E-6000 or stitch it on.

11. Add your Velcro dots to each end for a closure, making sure to measure the cuff around your wrist one final time for a good fit.

# FUSED PLASTIC BAG SHOE FLOWER

Most every girl I know has shoes with flowers on them. But none of them have a shoe with a *recycled* flower on it!

## Other Ideas for this Technique:

Hairpins, bracelets, rings, and appliqués for handbags or tote bags.

## YOU'LL NEED

- Plastic bags
- Scissors (try Fiskars pinking shears for added texture)
- Parchment paper
- Iron and ironing board or countertop
- Crystal beads or pearls or a big gem
- Needle and thread
- E-6000 glue

## HERE'S HOW

**1** Cut the handles and bottom off your plastic bags.

**2** Stack four flat pieces of plastic about the same size and sandwich them between two pieces of parchment paper.

**3** Experiment with your iron to get the right setting (see page 255) and gently iron over the parchment paper. Your bags will shrink a little bit, but shouldn't melt.

**4** Check after every few swipes of the iron to see if your bags are fusing together. If they're not, you may need to turn up the iron a little bit.

**5** Remove the fused plastic and cut out wavy circles or flower shapes.

**6** To give your flowers dimension, put each flower between layers of parchment paper, touch down with the iron, and immediately remove them. This wrinkles them a little bit.

*Optional:* I painted the edges of my black circular flower pieces with Jacquard Lumiere metallic paint in Pewter and I love the way it looks. Think about giving them a little bit of color to make them interesting.

**7** Stack your shapes from large to small.

**8** With a needle and thread, stitch up from the bottom and add a bead. Continue with as many beads as you want for the center of the flower.

**9** Glue the piece to your shoe with E-6000 or add a clip and make it a shoe clip.

# RECYCLED GOLD LEAF BRACELETS

Wait! Stop! Don't toss out that big plastic juice bottle! You can use it to make something beautiful and in a very tiny way, you can help save the earth. Every time you reuse something that could go in a landfill, you're doing your part to help. Can you imagine if we all did that every day?

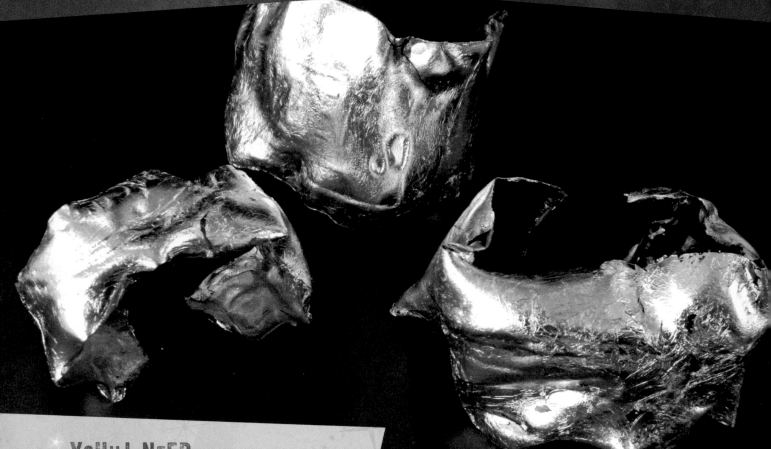

## YoU'LL NeeD

- Thick plastic juice bottle (I like Ocean Spray bottles)
- Scissors
- Newspaper or magazine pages
- 2 pairs of needle-nose pliers
- Embossing heat gun, hairdryer, or candle
- Lumiere Piñata Alcohol Inks in colors you like (see Resource Guide)
- Krylon spray adhesive
- 1 or 2 sheets of gold leaf or faux gold leaf
- ½-inch to 1-inch-wide flat paintbrushes
- Minwax Polycrylic clear coat

## HeRE's HoW

1. With scissors, cut off the top of the plastic bottle.

2. Cut the bottle into sections that look like very large bracelets. Don't worry if the sections look too big; they will shrink!

3. Holding your plastic bracelet with your needle-nose pliers, heat it and bend it into the perfect bangle shape. This is going to take some practice, but you'll get the hang of it. The more misshapen the better, I say.

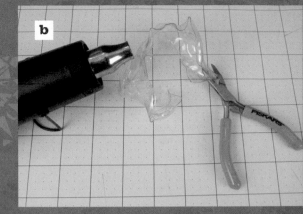

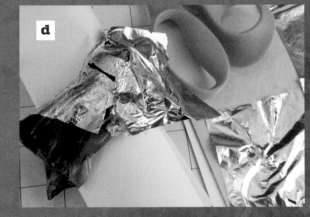

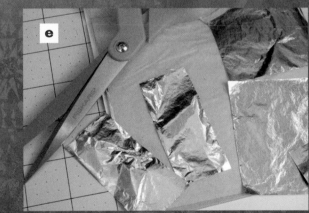

**4** Paint your bracelets with the alcohol inks and let dry.

**5** Roll up some newspaper or magazine pages and spray the outside of your bangle with spray adhesive.

**6** Carefully cut your gold leaf into sections about 1 inch by 2 inches wide.

**7** Using a dry flat paintbrush that has been rubbed through your hair to get a little static, pick up a section of gold leaf and apply it to the bracelet.

**8** Continue until your bracelet is covered with gold leaf.

**9** Coat your bracelet with Minwax Poly-crylic and let dry.

*Hint:*
DON'T WORRY if not every part of the bracelet is covered. It looks really neat with shots of color coming from underneath!

# SILVER AND GOLD

I've never really been a stickler about fashion rules. Rules are meant to be broken! Wear silver and gold together, for example. I think it looks just beautiful. Black and brown? Why not? Now, when your shoes don't match your belt, *that's* when I have a problem!

## YOU'LL NEED

- Flat, thin cardboard
- Scissors
- Elmer's Glue-All
- ICE Resin or Mod Podge Dimensional Magic
- Wax paper
- Drill with 1/16-inch drill bit
- Lumiere metallic paints in silver and gold
- Disposable paintbrushes
- 20 gold-tone jump rings
- Needle-nose pliers (and wirecutters if your pliers don't have them)
- 8 inches of medium gold-tone chain
- 1 gold-tone lobster claw closure
- Rubber or plastic gloves

## HERE'S HOW

**1** From the cardboard, cut three sets of four lopsided circles ½ inch to 1¾ inch in diameter.

**2** Cut four sets of three lopsided circles 1 inch to 1¾ inches in diameter.

**3** Cut four sets of two lopsided circles 1½ inches to 1¾ inches in diameter.

**4** Cut two plain circles 1¾ inches in diameter.

**5** Glue the two smallest circles together and your two largest circles together on your sets of four circles with Elmer's glue. If you're get confused (like I am right now), take a look at the photos!

**6** Glue the bottom two circles together on your four sets of three circles with Elmer's glue.

**7** Mix your resin outside using gloves.

**8** Lay your pieces down on wax paper. Coat all your pieces with the resin, then bring inside and let dry in an area of the house that you don't use. The fumes from resin can be harsh and you will need to work in a well-ventilated area.

**9** The next day, turn your pieces over, coat them again, and let dry.

**10** Paint all of your pieces either gold or silver and let dry.

**11** Lay your pieces down and lightly mark them where they need a hole drilled.

**12** Drill all of the holes in your pieces.

**13** Link your pieces together with jump rings.

**14** Cut two 4-inch pieces of chain and add them to the last circles with jump rings.

**15** Add jump rings to the ends of the chain and a lobster claw for the closure.

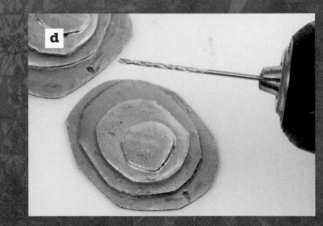

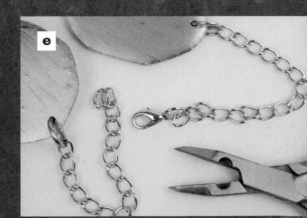

# TASTE OF SOUTHWEST SILVER

What could be more fun than wearing something bold and beautiful and then telling people that it's made entirely from discarded cardboard?! I say not much!

## YOU'LL NEED

- Flat, thin cardboard
- Scissors
- Elmer's Glue-All
- Clothespins
- Fiskars pinking shears
- ICE Resin
- Wax paper
- Paintbrush (for the paint and clear coat) and a disposable paintbrush (for the resin)
- Lumiere silver metallic paint
- Minwax Polycrylic or Minwax Clear Brushing Lacquer
- Rubber or plastic gloves
- *Optional:* X-ACTO knife

## HERE'S HOW

**1** Cut a strip of cardboard that measures 2½ to 3 inches by 9 inches. Rub it along the edge of a counter to give it flexibility. (Imagine that the cardboard is a curling ribbon, but you're using the edge of a counter instead of scissors.)

**2** Glue it in a bangle shape, making sure it's big enough to go over your hand comfortably. Use Elmer's glue to hold it in place while it dries with two clothespins.

**3** Cut strips ⅜ inch by 2½ inches with pinking shears. Glue them around the cuff with more Elmer's glue and let dry. Cut squares and rectangles—any shapes you want—using the patterns on page 366. Create any kind of design you want.

**4** If you need to, review the instructions on the ICE Resin and my tips on page 232. Mix your resin outside using gloves. Place your cuffs on wax paper and coat the pieces with the resin, making sure you get it everywhere

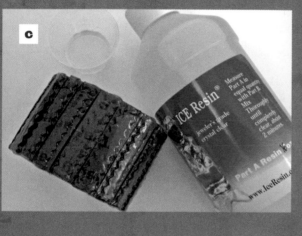

and that it's not drippy. This will make your cardboard pieces as strong as metal!

**Hint:**
If you do get drips or blobs, carefully shave them off with an X-ACTO knife. It's easy to do.

4 When the cardboard pieces are dry, paint them with the Lumiere silver and let them dry.

5 Coat the entire cuff with Minwax Polycrylic or Minwax Clear Aerosol Lacquer for a tough finish.

My obsession with costume dramas and Victorian clothing inspired me to write this chapter. I've always loved the jewelry that mourners wore to funerals in centuries past, but the concept of "mourning jewelry" just seemed too depressing! Thankfully, black jet is now fashionable (again), simply because it's so beautiful and chic! The best part about making projects for this chapter was spray-painting the pieces that didn't quite work in their original form. When my brooch necklace was too colorful, I sprayed it black, and it instantly looked wonderful. When my button clusters looked like, well, button clusters, I sprayed them and gave them a new life. Try it! You'll see what I mean.

# THREE TIER MOURNING CHOKER

I admit it. I'm hooked on period dramas. Give me *Pride and Prejudice* or *Monsieur Beaucaire* and I'm IN! Besides the clothes in these movies, I always notice the jewelry—especially when they have to attend a funeral. All the ornate pieces in jet black look just amazing. Now, when making this necklace, it doesn't really matter if you have black elements or not. Once you assemble your pieces, just spray paint them, and *voilà*, you've got the perfect piece to match your little black dress!

*Hint:*
Try spraying them in your favorite color and see what happens.

## YOU'LL NEED

- Two 7½-inch pieces of rosary bead chain
- Two ¼-inch pieces of silver or black chain
- Two 10-inch pieces of silver or black chain
- 24 inches of silver or black chain
- Needle-nose pliers
  (and wirecutters if the pliers don't have them)
- 1 large cheap earring or pendant
  (with holes so that you can add jump rings)
- 1 large (½-inch-diameter) black faceted bead
  (or bead of your choice)
- 5 silver or black jump rings
- 1 silver or black lobster claw closure
- Krylon Fusion for Plastic black spray paint

## HERE'S HOW

**1** Cut your chains. Gather any jewelry pieces and fittings together that aren't already black and spray-paint them. Make sure to get all sides.

**2** Create a tassel by cutting your 24-inch chain into seven to eight 3-inch pieces and join them with a jump ring.

**3** Add the 10-inch chain, the 8¼-inch chain, and then the 7½-inch chain to a jump ring on the ends of your necklace and a lobster claw for the closure.

**4** Gather them in the middle with another jump ring by adding the long chain first, then the shorter chain, and finally the beaded chain. You will begin to see how they form tiers.

**5** Hang your pendant or large earring from the center jump ring.

**6** Add your chain tassel to the bottom of the pendant or earring.

# BUTTON CLUSTER STATEMENT CHOKER

I actually made this choker for another book a long time ago but wasn't quite happy with it. Then it hit me—a little spray paint was all it needed! I used one crystal for this piece, but you could add more or paint it another color. I was taken with how chic the black looked, but like many, my tastes can change with the direction of the wind.

## YOU'LL NEED

- Aluminum flashing
- Tin shears or heavy-duty scissors with serrated blades
- Selection of about 30 buttons, mostly shank (the ones with the loop on the back)
- Needle-nose pliers (and wirecutters if the pliers don't have them)
- 6 inches of 18-gauge wire or 3 paper clips
- E-6000 glue
- 24 inches of small chain either black or silver (to create tassel)
- 16 inches of medium or large chain in black or silver (for around your neck)
- 5 gunmetal jump rings
- Krylon gray primer
- Krylon gloss or flat black
- Large crystal
- 1 gunmetal lobster claw closure

*Hint:*
www.createforless.com has an amazing selection of chain, and they carry black chain, too!

## HERE'S HOW

**1** Cut out a piece of aluminum flashing about 4 inches by 5 inches with tin shears or heavy-duty serrated scissors. Using the pattern on page 368, draw a fat crescent moon on your flashing, then cut out the crescent from the flashing.

**2** Clip off the backs of the shank buttons with wirecutters so they're flat.

a

b

c

d

e

**3** Cut three 2-inch pieces of wire (or use paper clips). Make 2-inch loops with the wire. Glue them to each pointed edge and to the center of the aluminum crescent with E-6000. You will use these loops to attach the neck chain and your hanging tassel.

**4** To create your button cluster centerpiece, glue all your buttons on the crescent with E-6000 in a pattern you like and let dry.

**5** Cut eight 3-inch pieces of the small chain and slip them onto a jump ring to create your tassel. If you're making this with silver chain, add the jump ring to the loop at the center of the crescent. If you're using small black chain, wait until you've spray-painted your button cluster to attach the tassel.

**6** Cut two 8-inch pieces of chain for the neck. If you're using silver chain, attach it to one of the loops on the side of your button cluster with two jump rings so you can paint the chain at the same time you paint your button cluster centerpiece. If you're using black chain, wait until you've painted your button cluster to attach it.

**7** Spray your pieces with the gray primer and let dry. Make sure to paint all parts of each piece.

**8** Spray-paint your pieces black and let dry.

**9** Glue on your crystal with E-6000.

**10** Add jump rings to the ends of the chain and a lobster claw for the closure.

# CLUSTER AND CRYSTAL CUFF

I've always loved buttons clustered on jewelry, gloves, and frames—I was obsessed with my grandmother's button tin when I was growing up. My challenge has always been to find enough buttons that look great together, so I figured out a simple way to make them match—spray paint! Feeling it still wasn't quite enough when I was done, I topped off this cuff with a big crystal to make it POP!

## YoU'LL NEED

- Wide metal cuff
- Wirecutters
- 25 to 30 shank buttons
  (the ones with the loop on the back)
- E-6000 glue
- Transparent tape
- Krylon gray primer
- Krylon flat black
- 1 large crystal button or stone

## HeRE's HoW

1. Using wirecutters, cut off the shanks on the backs of the buttons.

2. Glue your buttons on your cuff with E-6000, making sure to leave a space in the center of the cuff to place your crystal (but don't glue on your crystal just yet).

**Hint:**
To keep your buttons from slipping around, secure them with some transparent tape while they dry.

3. When the glue is dry, spray your entire cuff with gray primer and let dry.

4. Spray your cuff with flat black and let dry.

5. Glue your crystal in the center space and let dry.

6. Go out and impress!

# BROOCH-EMBELLISHED TUFF CUFF

She did it again! Auntie gave you another cheapo brooch from the dollar store for Christmas, and though you're grateful for the gesture and you adore her, you just can't wear it without hanging your head in shame. Well, here's your chance to turn it into something beautiful and it couldn't be easier.

## YOU'LL NEED

- Cheap metal brooch (you know, the ones with plastic stones that look awful even from a distance?)
- Needle-nose pliers (and wirecutters if the pliers don't have them)
- Wide metal cuff (I got mine at the dollar store)
- E-6000 glue
- Krylon gray primer
- Krylon black flat or gloss

## HERE'S HOW

1. Carefully clip or rip off the pin on the back of the brooch with your pliers or wirecutters.
2. Glue it on the center of your metal cuff with the E-6000 and let dry.
3. Spray the entire cuff with Krylon gray primer and let dry.
4. Spray with the Krylon black in high gloss or flat and let dry.
5. Show your favorite auntie how much you loved her gift.

# ODE TO ANNA SUI

I've always been an admirer of the fashion designer Anna Sui. She's got such an amazing sense of style and adores dramatic jet-black jewelry, just like me. This stunning choker would look amazing with a low scoop-neck dress or a white T-shirt. Either way, you can make this with just a few simple items.

## YOU'LL NEED

- 5 small brooches or 1 large brooch and 2 pairs of large earrings
- 2 pairs of needle-nose pliers
- Krylon gray primer
- 16 inches of chain (black if you can find it, if not, no big deal)
- Krylon high-gloss black spray paint
- 7 gunmetal jump rings
- 1 gunmetal lobster claw closure

## HERE'S HOW

1. Head to the dollar store or raid your jewelry box for your five jewelry pieces. Remove any earring wires, clips, and pin backs.

2. Spray your five pieces with gray primer, making sure to flip them over and spray the back too. Let them dry.

3. If you're not using black chain, spray your chain with a primer coat.

4. Spray paint your pieces with the high-gloss black and let dry.

5. Figure out the spacing for your necklace and attach the jewelry pieces with jump rings on the chain.

6. Add jump rings to the ends of the chain and a lobster claw for the closure.

# BUTTON CROSS AND CRYSTAL CUFF

I can't count the times I've tried to glue buttons on something in hopes of making it chic. It almost never used to work, but I think I finally found the secret with this cuff. Try spraying it a different solid color and see what happens!

## YOU'LL NEED

- 5 shank buttons (the ones with the loop on the back)
- Needle-nose pliers (and wirecutters if the pliers don't have them)
- Small hammer
- Transparent tape
- E-6000 glue
- Wide metal cuff
- Krylon gray primer
- Krylon black
- 20 inches of crystal chain
- *Optional:* Sandpaper

## HeRE's HoW

**1** Cut the shanks from the backs of the buttons with wirecutters to make them flat.

**2** Gently tap the back of each button to flatten it out.

*Hint:*

If some of the shank is left, you can sand them down or flatten them a bit with a small hammer. If you're using plastic shank buttons, you can clip the shanks and then easily sand them flat.

**3** Glue your buttons in a cross shape in the center of the cuff with E-6000. Position the cuff so that your buttons don't slide off while you're gluing them. You can also use some transparent tape to hold them in place while they dry. You may have to do the sides one at a time.

**4** When the glue is dry, spray your cuff with gray primer and let dry.

**5** Spray your cuff with the black and let dry.

**6** Cut your crystal chain in lengths to create starbursts. With dabs of E-6000 on a toothpick, carefully glue the crystal starbursts on the cuff and let dry.

**7** Circle the center button with more crystal chain.

I must have hundreds of small Buddhas and good-luck elephants sitting around my craft house! I keep buying them without knowing exactly what to do with them. Who can resist six tiny elephants for only a dollar? Not me, that's for sure. One day, in a fit of creativity, I started drilling holes in them. The first one became an incense burner. I turned another into a large bead. Once I figured out how to drill them without breaking them, I was in heaven. My favorite piece is perhaps the easiest to make in this entire book—the elephant ring on page 283. Just search for Buddha figurines on www.amazon.com if you have trouble finding them at your local dollar store or thrift shop.

# HAPPY HEARTS BUDDHA

Have you ever seen sets of these little Buddhas at the dollar store? I see them all of the time and always wonder what crafty magic I could make with them. I always buy them and line them up on my kitchen windowsill. One day I took a drill to one and figured out that it could be made into a large bead. How lucky for me! I guess my little Buddhas really do bring good luck! Lucky, playful, colorful, and happy. That's what this piece is all about. Wear it and just see how much good luck flows into your life!

## YOU'LL NEED

- 24 inches of ½-inch satin ribbon
- Scissors
- 16 inches of ⅜-inch gold-tone chain
- Needle-nose pliers (and wirecutters if the pliers don't have them)
- 1 Lucky Buddha
- 1 large and several smaller gold-tone jump rings (for the charms)
- Drill with ¹⁄₁₆-inch drill bit
- 2 gold-tone flathead jewelry pins
- 3 to 5 small jump rings
- 3 inches of long fringe (I used green)
- Several heart charms
- Hot glue gun and glue sticks
- Needle-nose pliers

## HERE'S HOW

1. Cut 24 inches of ribbon. Cut 16 inches of chain. Weave your ribbon in and out of the gold chain and tie knots on the end links to keep it in place.

2. Drill a hole in the bottom of the Buddha at an angle out toward the front as shown in photo c. Take your time with this.

3. Push one flathead pin through the drilled hole, cut off the excess, and create a loop so that it's secure and you can hang the large jump ring from it in step 7.

4. Roll your fringe around the other flathead pin and hot-glue it as you roll to secure it and make your tassel.

5. Cut the pin and create a loop at the top of your tassel as shown in photo g.

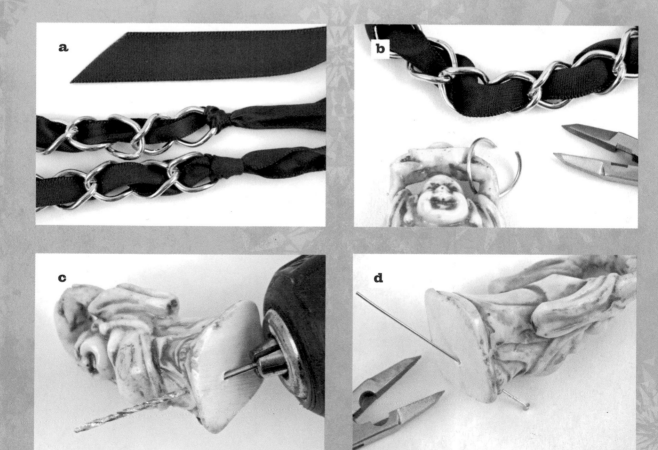

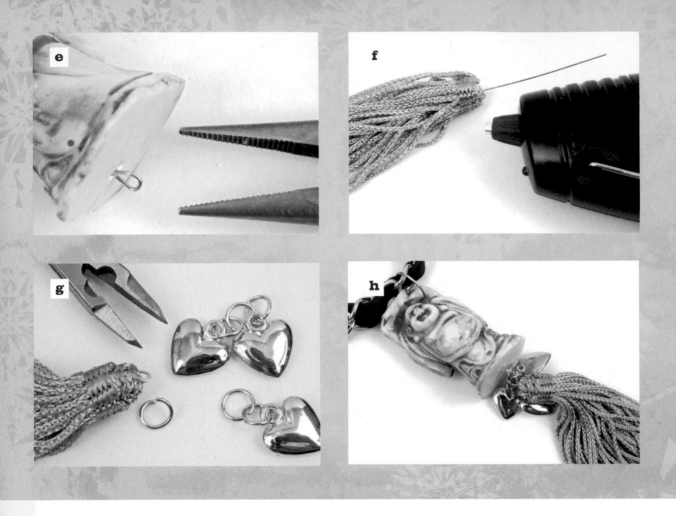

6  Attach small jump rings to your heart charms at the loop at the top of the tassel and hang the tassel from the loop at the bottom of the Buddha.

7  Attach the large jump ring to the chain and then hang your Buddha from it.

8  Tie the excess ribbon in a bow at the back of your neck for the closure.

# THERE'S AN ELEPHANT ON MY FINGER ✦

I couldn't resist this project. It was just too easy and way too fun. It reminded me that sometimes it's fun to wear something out of the ordinary just because you feel like it. Hit junk shops, Chinatowns, souvenir shops, or dollar stores for the perfect elephant or Buddha to turn into your lucky ring.

## YOU'LL NEED

- ◆ Small good-luck elephants (or Lucky Buddhas)
- ◆ Ring blank
- ◆ E-6000 glue

## HERE'S HOW

**1** Find a way to secure the elephant so the bottom is level. You can put it on a dish towel. Just make sure that it won't move while the glue is setting.

**2** Use a generous amount of E-6000 and let dry for a few hours.

# BUDDHA BOW

Buddhas, beads, and bows—what could be more perfect together? Hit the dollar store for sets of these little sculptures. I've been finding them everywhere. Whip out your drill and you've got the centerpiece for an amazing piece of jewelry. Not only that, you'll be carrying good luck around your neck. You could make this without the bow, but I thought it added a little something special to the piece. Mixing it up is what it's all about!

## YoU'LL NeeD

- Beading wire
- Needle-nose pliers (and wirecutters if the pliers don't have them)
- Crimp beads (gold or silver)
- 1 lobster claw closure
- Pearl beads
- 1 Lucky Buddha
- Drill with ¹⁄₁₆-inch drill bit
- 3 gold- or silver-tone jump rings
- 8 inches of 2-inch wide ribbon
- 8 inches of ¾-inch ribbon
- Scissors
- E-6000 glue
- Hot glue gun and glue sticks

## HeRE's HoW

1 Cut 18 inches of beading wire. Place a crimp bead on the end of the wire, loop it through the lobster claw, and back through the crimp bead. Crimp with your needle-nose pliers.

2 Drill a hole through the neck of your Buddha. (Wow, that sounds terrible, doesn't it?)

3 Add pearl beads and then the Buddha to the wire to create your necklace, making sure it's even on both sides.

4 Finish the necklace by adding a crimp bead and a jump ring, then looping the wire back through a crimp bead. Pull taut and crimp.

5 Cut 8 inches of the 2-inch ribbon and create your bow by folding over the ends so they meet in the center. Hot-glue them down.

6 Crimp the bow the way you want it to look and hot glue it in place.

7 Tie a knot around the center with the ¾-inch ribbon. Add a dab of hot glue if you feel like the knot will come undone.

8 Glue the bow to the underside of the Buddha with E-6000 and let dry.

# GOOD LUCK ELEPHANT CUFF

Yes, you're strong enough to lift en elephant. At least, that's what you should be thinking when you're wearing this piece, even if you feel the weight of the world on your shoulders.

a

b

c

## YOU'LL NEED

- 1 flat metal cuff
- Small elephant sculpture
- E-6000 glue
- Krylon gray primer
- Green seed beads (or any color you like)
- Lumiere metallic bronze paint (see Resource Guide)
- Paintbrush
- Elmer's Glue-All
- Minwax Polycrylic clear coat

d

## HERE'S HOW

**1** Glue your elephant on the center of the cuff with E-6000 and let dry.

**2** Spray the cuff thoroughly with gray primer.

**3** Paint the cuff with Lumiere metallic bronze (or any metallic color you like).

**4** Brush some Elmer's glue on your cuff around the elephant, sprinkle on some seed beads, and let dry.

**5** Repeat step 4 until you've added as many beads as you want.

**6** When the beads are dry and in place, coat them and the entire cuff in at least two coats of Minwax Polycrylic.

e

# LUCKY ELEPHANT

Did you know that only elephant sculptures that have their trunks up in the air are lucky? Also, if you have an elephant sculpture in your home, the trunk should be facing the door. Well, at least that's what I've heard. I was lucky enough to find these little pieces not only with their trunks in the air, but I also found the perfect place to hang a chain. Now that's lucky!

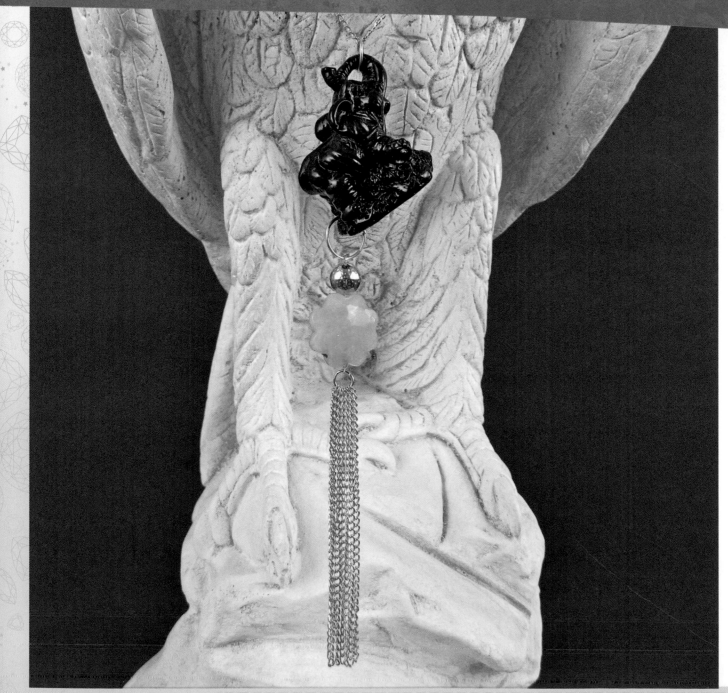

## YOU'LL NEED

- Small elephant figurine
- Drill with 1/16-inch drill bit
- Needle-nose pliers (and wirecutters if the pliers don't have them)
- Piece of scrap wood
- 72 inches of fine gold-tone chain (www.createforless.com has a terrific selection)
- 3 large gold-tone jump rings
- 3 inches of gold-tone beading wire or flathead pin
- Large jade bead or bead of your choice
- Small gold bead or bead of your choice

a

## HERE'S HOW

**1** Drill a hole in the base of the elephant and drill all the way through the figurine, from bottom out through the back at an angle using the drill bit. Do this on a scrap piece of wood so that you don't ruin your countertops or a nice piece of furniture!

**2** Cut ten 4-inch pieces of gold chain. Create your tassel by placing the chains on a jump ring.

**3** Place one large and one small bead on your gold wire and create loops on both ends with your needle-nose pliers.

**4** Hang your chain tassel from the end.

**5** Place a jump ring through the base of the elephant and hang your tassel from the jump ring.

**6** Thread the 32-inch chain through the elephant at the top and close with a jump ring to finish the necklace.

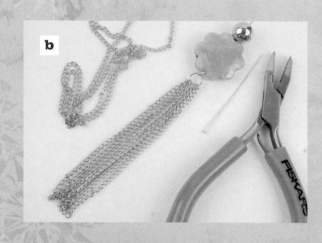

b

c

### Hint:
If you don't have a hole made near the trunk like I do, you can simply drill a hole through the top, too. If this is the case, you will need an extra jump ring or a hole big enough for the fine chain to go through.

d

# SIMPLY CHARMING

**Y**ou know what puts me in a terrific mood? Bling. More specifically, lots of charms and goodies hanging from a necklace or choker. Whether you use crosses, tassels, or random danglers you've collected at the bottom of your jewelry box, these next few pieces are sure to make a statement and get the conversation going.

# CROSS MY HEART

Eat your heart out, Madonna! Since wearing crosses has become a fashion statement, I thought I would take advantage of the MANY offerings at my local dollar store. I can't think of a better way to keep away an army of vampires and look chic at the same time.

## YoU'LL NeED

- 10 to 12 different cross necklaces and rosaries
- Needle-nose pliers (and wirecutters if the pliers don't have them)
- 44 inches of large silver chain
- Silver-tone jump rings (enough for your charms)

## HeRE's HoW

**1** Remove the crosses from all the necklaces.

**2** Create a multistrand set of chains with the chains. Cut two 22-inch pieces of the large chain and add them to the strands. Make sure all of the chains are large enough to fit over your head.

**3** Connect all the chains at the back with jump rings.

**4** Start adding crosses to the chains one at a time to create a design that you like. In my design, I used the larger crosses in the middle and worked the smaller crosses up the sides.

# CRYSTAL TASSEL TRIO

I showed this to a friend of mine and she basically told me that she liked everything but the tassels. (We're not friends anymore.) Perhaps if I had told her I called it the Crystal Tassel Trio, she would have understood it was the point of the piece. A week later I took off the tassels and realized that she may have had a point. You could really just stop before adding the tassels and still have an amazing necklace. Maybe I should give her a call?

## You'll Need

- Gunmetal chains of various thicknesses (enough for five 16-inch strands)
- Needle-nose pliers (and wirecutters if the pliers don't have them)
- 27 gunmetal jump rings
- 1 large gunmetal lobster claw closure
- 20 crystal beads
- 3 black cord tassels
- 1 brooch (2-inch-diameter)
- Krylon high-gloss black spray paint
- 25 flathead gunmetal jewelry pins

## Here's How

**1** Cut five 16-inch strands from your various gunmetal chains. Create your chain base by attaching the five chains to a jump ring at each end and a lobster claw on one side for the closure.

**2** Create your crystal charms by placing a crystal on a flathead pin, cutting off the excess wire, and creating a loop with your needle-nose pliers.

**3** Working with three chains, hang the charms with jump rings at various places on the necklace.

**4** Push a flathead pin through the center of each tassel up through the top, add a crystal bead, cut off the excess, and bend a loop with your needle-nose pliers.

**5** Spray-paint the brooch black and let dry.

**6** Hang one tassel from the bottom center of the brooch with a jump ring and pin the brooch in the center of all five chains, going through several loops to keep it together.

**7** Hang the other two tassels evenly on both sides of the center brooch with jump rings.

*Note:*
I got my tassels at www.createforless.com, but you could just as easily make your own! Check out my instructions on pages 16–17.

# GAMBLER'S GOOD LUCK

Next time you head to Las Vegas, this is the necklace I think you should wear. I found all these terrific colorful dice at the dollar store and was able to drill a hole in them quite easily. Make a shorter version to create a bracelet, and if you win big, make sure to send me a cut! Remember to check the Resource Guide for unusual jewelry supplies and novelties.

## YOU'LL NEED

- Gold-tone chains of various sizes (enough for five strands of 22 to 26 inches)
- Needle-nose pliers (and wirecutters if the pliers don't have them)
- 26 gold-tone jump rings
- 1 gold-tone lobster claw closure
- 12 dice
- Drill with 1/16-inch drill bit
- Scrap wood
- 20 crystal beads
- 12 (3-inch) flathead jewelry pins
- 16 inches of dark green crystal chain (or any color you like)
- 16 inches of light green crystal chain (or any color you like)
- 4 flat eyes from hook and eye sets

## HeRE's HoW

**1** Cut five strands of gold-tone chains ranging from 22 to 26 inches long. Attach your multi-strand necklace base in the back with jump rings and a lobster claw for the closure.

**2** Drill holes in all of your dice with your drill and small drill bit. Do this on some scrap wood so you don't ruin your countertop or work surface.

**3** Create your dice and crystal charms by placing a crystal and then the dice on a flathead pin, cutting off the excess, and looping with your needle-nose pliers.

**4** Attach the dice to the chains in various places with jump rings.

**5** Cut 16 inches from each of your colored crystal chains. Glue the flat eyes to each end of the crystal chains and let dry. Using jump rings, attach the flat eyes at the ends of your crystal chains to the gold chains by weaving them in and out to create a loosely braided look as shown in photo e. You want it to look a little jumbled.

**6** Create crystal charms by placing crystals on flathead pins, cutting off the excess, and creating loops with your needle-nose pliers. Hang them where you like with jump rings.

# ONE-OF-A-KIND JEWELRY CHARMER

It's time to forage and gather some trinkets, key chains, and game parts that have been hanging around the house. You're going to make a choker that would easily sell for a few hundred dollars in any boutique. The great thing about this piece is that no one else will have the selection of unique items you use—it's guaranteed to be one-of-a-kind. Aren't you one-of-a-kind already anyway? I think your accessories should be, too.

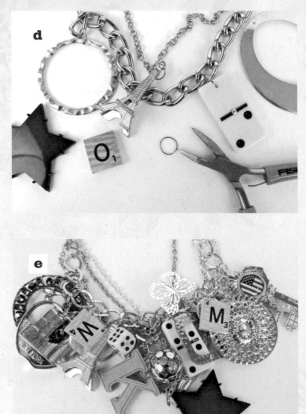

## YOU'LL NEED

- Old jewelry, key chains, charms, game pieces, dominos . . .
- Drill with 1/16-inch drill bit
- Silver- or gold-tone chain in different sizes
- About 30 silver- or gold-tone jump rings
- Needle-nose pliers (and wirecutters if the pliers don't have them)
- 1 silver- or gold-tone lobster claw closure

## HERE's HOW

**1** Gather all the fun pieces you can find—the sky's the limit—dice, dominos, Scrabble pieces, old jewelry, magnetic letters . . . Take apart the jewelry and see whether the pieces have holes in them.

**2** Drill a hole in all your pieces that don't already have one.

**3** Cut the chains the length you want for your necklace, and as many as you want. Connect your chains with jump rings at the ends, either leaving two longer ends for the neck or cutting two equal lengths to make the back. This will vary depending on the chains you have. Add jump rings and a lobster claw for the closure.

**4** Start adding your pieces one by one until you get the look you want. Remember, MORE IS BETTER! This is *not* a case where less is more.

**A**luminum flashing saved my life. I first found it on a roll at the hardware store, and once I figured out that you could very easily cut it with tin shears or heavy-duty serrated scissors, I was hooked. Anytime I want to make something that I know will last forever, I make it out of tin. And if I want to mount something or create a backing, I know the answer: TIN! Make sure to wear cotton gloves when cutting tin, as the tiny scrap pieces can be sharp.

# THE TIN IS "IN"

I really love playing around with spray paint in the backyard. I'd say it's a daily event for me since I started writing craft books. This necklace happened by accident when I began looking at my spray-paint station. It was filled with so many different colors, and somehow it looked perfect. I wanted to capture that random explosion of color on a necklace that someone could wear with almost anything, and this is what happened.

## FOR THE NECKLACE YOU'LL NEED

- Aluminum flashing
- Tin shears or heavy-duty scissors with serrated edges
- Hammer and nail
- Scrap wood
- Several different colors of Krylon spray paint
- Newspaper or magazine page
- Krylon Acrylic Crystal clear coat spray
- 6 gold-tone jump rings
- 12 inches of gold-tone chain (your choice)
- Needle-nose pliers (and wirecutters if the pliers don't have them)
- 1 gold-tone lobster claw closure

*Hint:*
Serrated edges cut the tin with a tiny jagged edge so that the metal is not sharp and won't cut you. Very important!

## HERE'S HOW

**1** Cut a piece of aluminum flashing about 10 inches by 10 inches. Using the patterns on page 372, trace and cut out your shapes in the flashing. Be careful because it can be sharp. If you have cotton gloves, wear them!

**2** With your hammer and nail, tap a hole in the top and bottom of the square, in the sides and bottom center of the crescent shape, and tap one hole near the edge of the circle. Do this on a piece of scrap wood to protect your countertop or work surface.

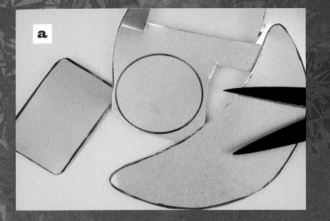

a

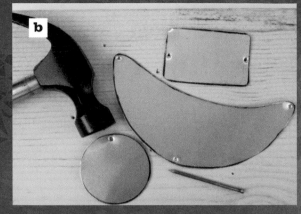

b

c

d

**3** Flip your pieces over and tap down any sharp edges.

**4** Spray-paint your pieces a base color (I chose red).

**5** Lightly spray other colors on top of the red, layering them and letting them splatter to get the effect you want.

**6** Crunch up a newspaper or magazine page into a ball. Spray some paint on another magazine page and dab the ball into the paint, then dab it onto your pieces to add more texture.

**7** Let your pieces dry and repeat the dabbing technique on the back of the tin pieces.

**8** Spray all the pieces thoroughly in Krylon Crystal Clear Acrylic and let dry.

**9** Attach your pieces together with jump rings.

**10** Cut your chain in two 6-inch pieces. Attach them to the ends of the crescent shape with jump rings.

**11** Attach jump rings and a lobster claw for the closure.

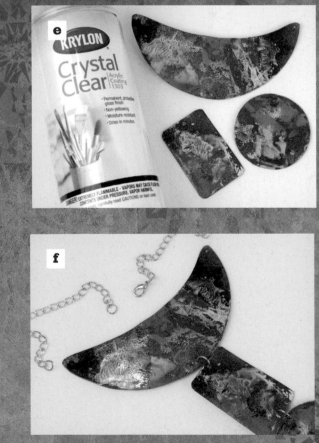

e

f

## FOR THE EARRINGS
## YOU'LL NEED

- All items needed for the necklace above (except chain and lobster claw)
- 4 gold-tone jump rings
- 2 gold-tone earring wires

## HERE'S HOW

**1** Using the patterns on page 372 and following the instructions for the necklace, cut out four circles in two different sizes (two in each size) from aluminum flashing.

**2** Following the instructions for the necklace, paint the pieces and let dry.

**3** Tap two holes in the larger circles on opposite ends.

**4** Tap one hole near an edge in the smaller circles.

**5** Attach both sets of different-size circles together with a jump ring.

**6** Attach an earring wire with another jump ring and dangle away.

# EMBOSSED BUTTERFLIES

These pieces are so light and airy, they might actually just flutter away. Be careful, or they'll take you along with them! You can use any rubber stamp and any color combination you want for this project. I'd love to see what you come up with!

## YoU'll NeED

- Aluminum flashing
- Tin shears or heavy-duty scissors with serrated blades
- Rubber stamps
- Stamp pad
- Hammer and nail
- Scrap wood
- Flat black Krylon spray paint
- Gold embossing powder and embossing pad (see Resource Guide)
- Embossing heat gun or hot hairdryer
- 2 gold-tone earring wires (for the earrings)
- 2 gold-tone jump rings
- Needle-nose pliers

## FOR THE NECKLACE

- All the above (except earring fittings) plus:
- 1 large bead
- 1 gold-tone flathead pin
- 32 inches of small gold-tone chain
- Wirecutters if the pliers don't have them
- 6 gold-tone jump rings
- 1 gold-tone lobster claw closure

## HeRE's HoW

**1** Cut a rectangle 6 inches by 8 inches from the aluminum flashing with tin shears or heavy-duty serrated scissors. Make a stamp of the image you want to use on the flashing. Don't worry if the stamp isn't perfect; you just need to know the exact size to cut your tin pieces.

**2** Cut out your stamped images from the flashing, adding a small border (less than ¼ inch) all the way around.

**3** Tap a hole on the ends where you will be placing either your chains or your earring wires using the hammer and nail. Use scrap wood to protect your countertop or work surface. Flip the pieces over to tap the holes again and make sure there are no sharp edges around the hole.

**4** Spray-paint both sides of the tin pieces with flat black and let dry.

**5** Using the embossing pad, stamp your image again on the black tin piece, and while it's still wet, sprinkle embossing powder on top so it sticks to the image. Shake or lightly blow off the excess.

**6** Emboss your image with the heat gun or a very hot hairdryer.

**7** For the earrings, fit jump rings through the holes and attach earring wires.

**8** For the necklace, place the bead on a flathead pin, cut off the excess, and make a loop at the top of the pin.

**9** Cut two 16-inch pieces of chain. Join a double strand of chain to each side of the main butterfly (or stamped image) with a jump ring.

**10** Add jump rings at the ends of the chains and a lobster claw for the closure.

**11** Hang another stamped piece below that, then the large bead below that.

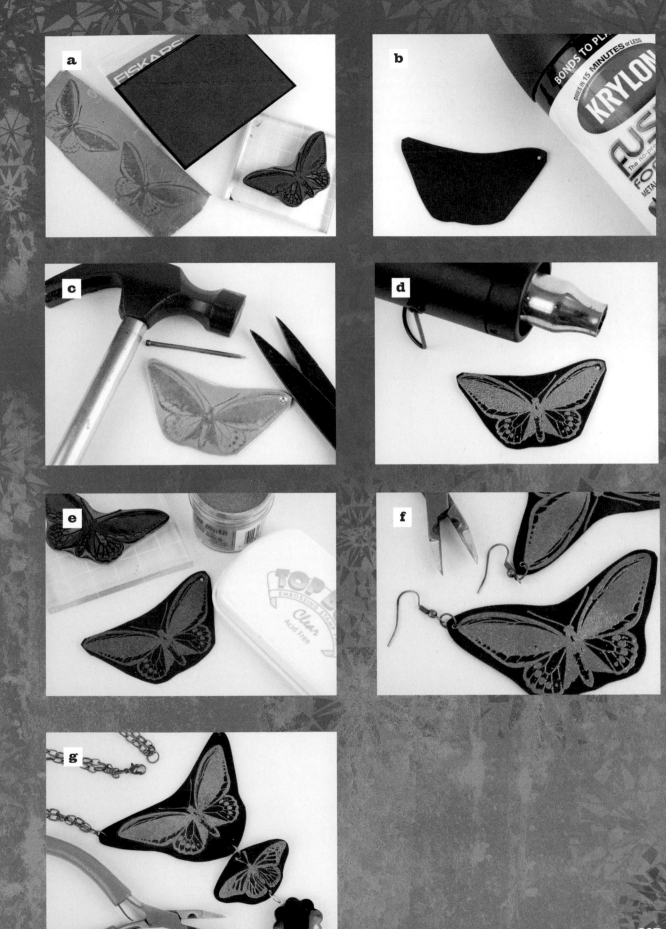

# ALL OVAL THE PLACE

I've said it a thousand times. I love a lady in big jewelry. Big jewelry means big fun, and I'm never wrong about this! You can make this piece any size you want, but I had to go all out. And the next time you're at a party, look for the lady with the big jewelry and hang out with her. She'll be the most fun.

## YoU'LL NeED

- ◆ Aluminum flashing
- ◆ Tin shears or heavy-duty scissors with serrated blades
- ◆ Hammer and nail
- ◆ Scrap wood
- ◆ Krylon Glitter Blast in Silver Flash
- ◆ 8 inches of silver-tone chain
- ◆ 1 silver-tone lobster claw closure
- ◆ 15 large silver-tone jump rings
- ◆ Needle-nose pliers (and wirecutters if the pliers don't have them)

## HeRE's HoW

**1** Using tin shears or heavy-duty serrated scissors, cut out a piece of aluminimum flashing 10 inches by 10 inches. Trace ovals and circles from the patterns on page 369 onto the flashing and cut them out.

**2** With your hammer and nail, tap holes into each of the pieces according to the patterns. Use a piece of scrap wood to protect your countertop and work surface.

**3** After you tap your holes, flip each piece over and flatten the hole with your hammer by gently tapping the edges. This will eliminate any sharp edges.

**4** Lay your pieces out on newspaper and spray them with Silver Flash Glitter Blast and let dry.

**5** Flip the pieces over and paint the backs.

**6** Using the finished photo as a guide, link your metal pieces together with jump rings.

**7** Cut two 4-inch pieces of chain and connect them to each end of your necklace with a jump ring and finish the ends with jump rings and a lobster claw for the closure.

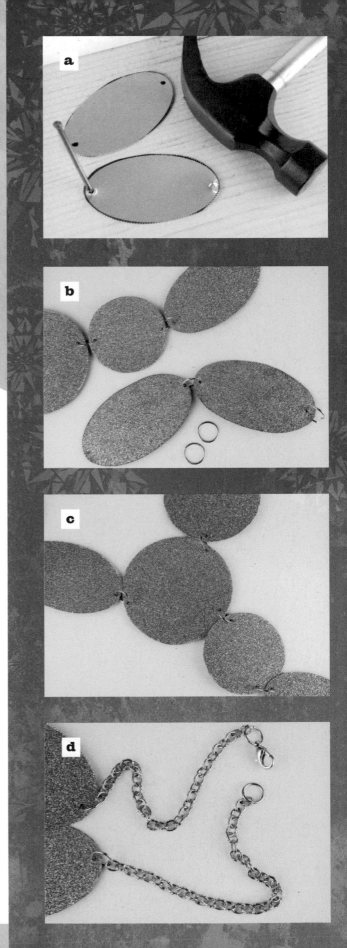

# WHAT TO WEAR!

hese pieces are a shout-out to my days as a fashion designer. Nothing was off-limits when I was creating for collections, and whatever I could dream up ended up walking down the runway. It was a joyous time of my life that I will always think about with a huge smile on my face.

# SIMPLE BUTTON CUFF LINKS

Nothing says chic like cuff links. They make any man or woman look polished and smart. If you ever see expensive buttons that you just have to buy but you're not sure what to do with them, this is a terrific project to use them for. You only have to buy two, so don't feel guilty about spending too much!

## YOU'LL NEED

- 2 inches of medium chain in a metal tone that matches your buttons
- 2 pairs of needle-nose pliers (and wirecutters if the pliers don't have them)
- 2 small shank buttons (the ones with loops on the back) that fit through a shirt buttonhole
- 2 larger shank buttons

## HERE'S HOW

1. Cut a section of about 4 links of chain, or about ½ inch.

2. Carefully open the end link using both pairs of your needle-nose pliers and close it around the shank of one of your buttons. I like to start with the smaller buttons first; it's easier.

3. Carefully open the link at the other end of the small piece of chain and close it around the shank of the larger button.

4. That's it!

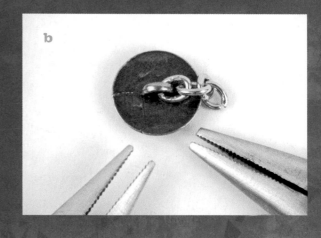

# A SHOULDER ABOVE THE REST

I thought this was a great way to add interest to a simple jacket, giving it a couture look without going over the top (so to speak). Most of us have something in our closet that could use some spark. I'll bet you have a few pieces of junk jewelry that could use a coat of spray paint, too. It's time to rework your wardrobe with some things you probably already have. Get to it!

## YoU'LL NeED

- Blazer or jacket that needs some love
- 5 inexpensive brooches
- 42 inches of medium chain
- Wirecutters
- Krylon gray primer
- Krylon black Fusion for Plastic

## HeRE's HoW

**1** Clean your brooches and make sure they are free of dirt and dust.

**2** Spray them with the gray primer and let dry.

**3** Spray-paint them black and let dry. (But why not spray them a different color like bright red or coral? Just a thought.)

**4** Cut 42 inches of chain and loop the ends on the pin backs of two of the brooches, then pin them on your jacket so that the chain drapes between them. I like one on the lapel and one near the shoulder.

**5** Pin the other brooches around the first two in a pattern you like.

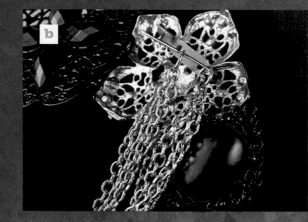

*Suggestion:*
Instead of black, try using your favorite color of spray paint for this project.

# ANTIQUE PEARL AND CHAIN NECKTIE

The perfect alternative to a necklace, I say. I wanted to come up with something that might inspire you to use a collar from an old shirt, and perhaps create a piece of antique fancy that might look good with a suit jacket and conservative blouse. So, with this project, you get two pieces for the price of one!

## YoU'LL NeED

- 63 inches of small to medium gold-tone chain
- Old blouse that you can cut apart
- Scissors
- Needle-nose pliers (and wirecutters if the pliers don't have them)
- 35 to 40 pearl beads (I chose purple and pink)
- 35 to 40 gold-tone flathead pins
- 3 gold-tone jump rings
- 2-inch-wide antique brass stamped filigree oval (check out www.vintagejewelrysupply.com)
- E-6000 glue
- Pin back

a

b

c

d

e

## HERE'S HOW

**1** Carefully cut the collar (with the collar band) off your blouse with your scissors. Make sure to remove all the extra threads.

**2** Cut the chain into seven pieces ranging between 7 and 9 inches.

**3** Place a pearl bead on a flathead pin and cut off the excess, leaving about ⅜ inch, then loop it around a link of chain.

**4** Continue until your chains are filled with pearls, making sure to add a pearl at the bottom of each chain. This will give it a more finished look.

**5** Attach three pearled chains to a jump ring and attach the jump ring in the center of your filigree oval at the bottom.

**6** Attach two pearled chains to a jump ring, then attach them to the right and left of the center chains.

**7** Bead a pearl on a flathead pin, thread it through the center of the oval, and make a loop at the back of the oval to secure it in place.

**8** Glue the pin on the back with E-6000 and let dry.

# BEAUTIFUL NO-SEW-BOW SHOE CLIPS

Any pair of basic black pumps can look formal and amazing with beautiful bow shoe clips. No need for a sewing machine. It's just a little hot-glue magic!

## YOU'LL NEED

- 9 inches of 2-inch grosgrain (ribbed) ribbon
- Scissors
- Iron
- Hot glue gun and glue sticks
- Feathers of your choice
- 2 clip-on earring blanks
- E-6000 glue
- Large flat-back crystal gem

## HeRE's HoW

1. Cut a 3-inch piece of ribbon and iron it in thirds to make a thin strip. This will be the center of the bow.

2. Cut a 6-inch piece of ribbon and hot-glue the ends to the center of the first ribbon as shown in photo d. This is the bow.

3. Pinch the bow and use tiny dabs of hot glue to keep it in place.

4. Carefully wrap the ironed piece around the pinched bow and secure it in the back. Fold the end over so it's neat and tidy.

5. Glue feathers on the front of your bow and then a crystal over the feathers with E-6000 and let dry.

6. Hot-glue the clip-on earring to the back of the bow, making sure to glue on the part with the hole in it, not the flat disk part. (It's flipped around so it will work as a shoe clip. The flat disk will clip under your shoe and should lie comfortably against your foot.)

# SHIMMERY SLANTED DAGGERS SKIRT

This easy technique can take a simple black skirt from plain to absolutely amazing with just a little time and a whole lotta safety pins. Pair this with a simple knit top and some amazing shoes and you'll look like you just walked off the pages of *Vogue*.

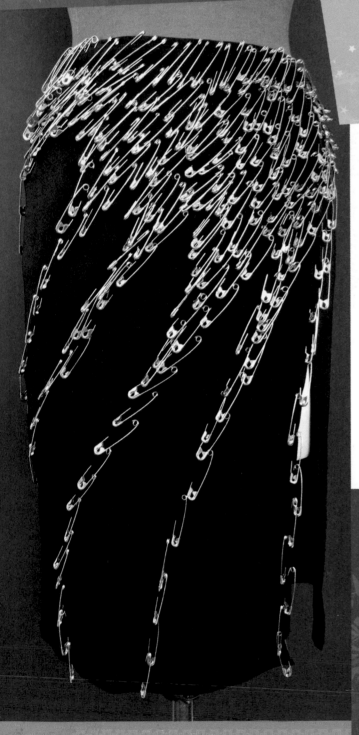

## YOU'LL NEED

- Black skirt
- 600 large (no. 3) safety pins
- Tailor's chalk

## HERE'S HOW

**1** Decide how you would like the design on your skirt to look. I chose slanted daggers. Lay your skirt flat on a table and play with the safety pins until you get a design you like. Don't worry too much—they're just pinned in and you can always change it.

**2** Mark out your design with the chalk. It will come off, but still, mark your skirt lightly.

**3** Starting at the waistband and keeping all of your safety pins at an angle, work your way across. Make sure to keep all of the pins uniform and about the same distance apart.

**4** Continue down the skirt at a slant, keeping the daggers wider at the top and working down to one pin at the hem.

# CRYSTAL SLIDER BROOCH BELT

Ever wonder what to do with those slider belt buckles that keep piling up in your belt drawer? Consolidate the belts, since they all fit on the same changeable buckle, and use the rest of the buckles for a project like this!

## YoU'LL NeED

- 2 yards of 2-inch grosgrain (ribbed) ribbon
- Scissors
- 2 yards of crystal chain
- Needle-nose pliers (and wirecutters if the pliers don't have them)
- 1 slider buckle
- Gem brooch that fits over your buckle
- E-6000 glue
- *Optional:* Sewing machine

## HeRE's HoW

**1** Figure out your waist measurement and add about 8 inches to the measurement for your belt. Cut the ribbon that length.

If you feel like your ribbon isn't thick enough, you can sew two pieces together to make your belt and that usually does the trick. I like to sew two layers together.

**2** Figure out exactly how tight you want your belt. (Once you glue on your crystal chain, it won't be able to slip through the slider part of the belt.) For example, if your waist is exactly 28 inches, then you need two lengths of crystal chain, each 26 inches long. Cut the crystal chain to the length you need.

**3** Using a very thin line of E-6000, glue your crystal chain to the ribbon, starting at the end that is attached to your slider buckle under the teeth (not the end you pull through the buckle).

**4** Remove the pin back from the brooch with your needle-nose pliers or wirecutters.

**5** Glue the brooch on top of the buckle with E-6000.

# BOW AND BROOCH BELT

I must have at least ten ribbon belts with slider belt buckles that I don't wear, and even if I did wear them, I only need one belt buckle for all of them, because they are all the same size. I needed to figure out something to do with all of these buckles since they were just itching for a project. And *voilà!* Here's what I came up with!

## YoU'LL NeED

- 3 yards of 2-inch grosgrain (ribbed) ribbon
- Scissors
- 2 yards of crystal chain
- Wirecutters
- Hot glue gun and glue sticks
- 1 slider buckle
- Gem brooch
- E-6000 glue
- *Optional*: Sewing machine

## HeRE's HoW

**1** Figure out your waist measurement and add about 8 inches to the measurement for your belt. Cut the ribbon that length. If you feel like your ribbon isn't thick enough, you can sew two pieces together to make your belt and that usually does the trick. I like to sew two layers together.

**2** Figure out exactly how tight you want your belt. (Once you glue on your crystal chain, it won't be able to slip through the slider part of the belt.) For example, if your waist is exactly 28 inches, you need two lengths of crystal chain, each 26 inches long.

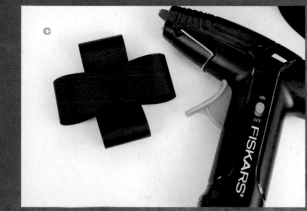

**3** Using a very thin line of E-6000, attach your crystal chain to the ribbon, starting at the end that is attached to the slider buckle under the teeth (not the end you pull through the buckle).

**4** Cut your ribbon into four 8-inch pieces.

**5** Create the bow by hot-gluing the ends of each piece to the center.

**6** Glue the four pieces in a crisscross with more hot glue.

**7** Remove the pin back from the brooch with the wirecutters,

**8** Glue the brooch on top of the bow with E-6000.

**9** Glue the bow and brooch centerpiece on top of the slider buckle with a generous amount of E-6000.

# BOW AND BROOCH CLUTCH

I know you must have at least three wallets in your closet that need some love and attention. You don't want to toss them, because you just know that *one day* you'll use them again, right? Well, with a little glitter blast and some ribbon, you *will* use them again. I promise!

## YoU'LL NeED

- 1 yard of 2-inch black grosgrain (ribbed) ribbon
- 1 yard of ½-inch gray satin ribbon
- Scissors
- Hot glue and glue gun
- 1 gem brooch
- E-6000 glue
- Wallet in need of a makeover
- Krylon gray primer
- Krylon Glitter Blast in Starry Night
- Minwax Clear Aerosol Lacquer
- Masking tape
- 1 black cord tassel (see Resource Guide)

## HeRE's HoW

1. Cut the black ribbon and gray ribbon each into four 8-inch pieces.

2. Hot-glue the ends of each ribbon to the center point of each ribbon.

3. Hot-glue the ribbons on top of each other in a crisscross formation to create a flat bow.

4. Hot-glue the gray bow on top of the black bow.

5. Glue the brooch on top of both bows with E-6000.

6. Tape over the zipper on your clutch and then spray it on both sides with gray primer, and let dry.

7. Spray the clutch with the Glitter Blast on each side and let dry.

8. Spray the clutch with Minwax Clear Aerosol Lacquer and let dry. This is the best-kept secret for keeping spray-painted objects from remaining tacky. It will also give you an amazing finish and keep your glitter intact.

9. Glue the bow and brooch centerpiece on the center of your clutch with a generous amount of E-6000 and let dry.

# FEATHER EPAULETTES

When I started writing this book, I headed to the thrift store (as I always do when I start a new book), and I found this jacket. It had a nice shape and it was in terrific condition. It stayed on my dress form for nearly a month before I started playing with it. At first there were just chains, and over time I had added enough different items to it to make Lady Gaga swoon. This piece, worn with black tights and boots, would make a KILLER outfit. It's also a great way to give new life to an old favorite.

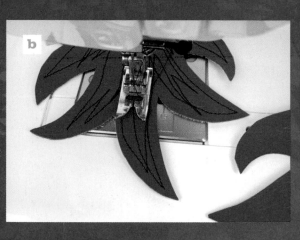

## You'll Need

- Red vinyl or leather
- Scissors
- Sewing machine with black thread
- Grommet maker and 12 gold grommets (these are sold at most sewing-supply stores)
- E-6000 glue
- 2 feather hackle pads in red or black (www.createforless.com)
- 8 yards of fine to medium gold-tone chain
- 4 pin backs
- 12 gold-tone jump rings

## Here's How

1. Cut a piece about 6 inches by 14 inches from your red vinyl or leather. Cut out flames using the pattern on page 373.

2. On your sewing machine, stitch a pattern onto them in black thread to give them some interest. (If you don't have a sewing machine or choose to skip this step, that's okay, too.)

3. Punch grommets along the vinyl in the places indicated by the pattern.

4. Glue the entire vinyl flame piece to the top of the feather hackle pad with E-6000 and let dry.

5. Flip over and glue two pin backs to the underside with E-6000.

6. Pin the piece on your jacket shoulder and drape the chains from the front of the jacket to the back. Attach with jump rings in the grommet holes.

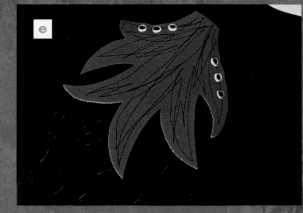

# SHRUFFLE (SHRUG WITH RUFFLES)

I thought for a brief, wonderful moment that I had invented a new word . . . but then I found it on Google. It doesn't have the same definition, but sadly, it's out there. But I'll still be happy knowing that this is a different definition for a very fun word. This "shruffle" is a supereasy way to create a couture look for very little money. Change the fabrics and the colors, and soon you'll have a piece that has everyone asking you where you shop.

## You'll Need

- Old blouse that you can cut apart
- Scissors
- Fiskars pinking shears
- 2 yards of 1-inch ribbon to match your color palette
- 2 yards taffeta (your choice of colors)
- 2 yards organza
- Sewing machine with thread to match your colors
- 3½-inch-diameter drinking glass or circle stencil
- Hot glue gun and glue sticks

## Here's How

1. Cut the collar off your blouse with your regular scissors, keeping a low V-neck shape, and then cut your shirt just below the bustline (or at any length you are comfortable with).

2. Cut off your sleeves right at the seam so you have a short vest.

3. Measure around the bottom hem of your vest. Cut off that amount of ribbon plus a little extra, and stitch the ribbon around the bottom hem on the machine. If you need to, gather it a little bit under the bust for a better fit. You can do this by making little darts, or pleats—make sure to do it on both sides symmetrically so your garment lies even.

4. Cut about 120 organza circles and 120 taffeta circles about 3½ inches in diameter using the pinking shears.

5 Put an organza circle on top of a taffeta circle, fold in half twice, and stitch down in the center to make a ruffle.

6 Once you've made about 50 of these, start hot-gluing them on your vest until it's completely covered.

7 Add more if there are bald spots.

*Hint:*
Hot glue works
well with fabric because
it is porous.

# JUST ENOUGH CUFF

rap your wrist in these blingy pieces to add the perfect punctuation mark to your outfit. I have a friend named Sara who can wear 30 bracelets at the same time, and they look amazing on her. She has extra-long arms, and for some reason she decided this was her look. It totally works. Bracelets and cuffs are those fashion staples that people have been wearing since the dawn of time, and I'm just going to continue the tradition.

# CHANEL-INSPIRED CUFFS

I was at a cocktail party once at the home of a very wealthy woman, in a high-rise in New York City. I can't even remember how I got invited, but there I was, in this beautiful mansion in the sky. During the evening the hostess came up to me and said, "So you're a fashion designer? I'd like to show you something." She took me into her bedroom and showed me her closet, and I almost fell right out of that 30-story building. There was literally a mile of Chanel suits and dresses, and drawers full of Chanel jewelry. It was like a museum, and I have never seen anything like it in my entire life. From vintage garments to pieces with the tags still on them—she had it all. These cuffs are inspired by that evening.

## YOU'LL NEED

- (Large) 2½-inch silver-tone cuff
- (Small) 2-inch flat silver-tone metal cuff
- Krylon white primer
- Krylon Crème spray paint
- 2 yards of Mardi Gras pearls (the strands that are attached with string and can't move)
- 1½ yards of crystal chain
- Wirecutters
- E-6000 glue
- Toothpicks
- Large flat-back crystal gem (for the smaller cuff)

## HERE'S HOW
## TO MAKE THE LARGE CUFF

1. Spray the large cuff with white primer and let dry.

2. Spray with the Krylon Crème and let dry.

3. Cut lengths of pearls and chain that measure the width of your cuff.

4. With dabs of E-6000 on a toothpick, carefully glue a row of pearls straight across the metal cuff right in the center and let dry.

5. Now add a row of crystal chain.

6. Continue until the entire cuff is covered.

## FOR THE SMALLER CUFF

1. Glue your flat-back crystal to the center of the cuff and let dry.

2. Wrap pearls around the stone and cut to length. With dabs of E-6000 on a toothpick, carefully glue the pearls around your stone.

3. Cut crystal chain to fit alongside the pearls and glue onto the cuff.

4. Continue to alternate a row of pearls and then a row of crystals until your bracelet is covered.

# CELEBRATION CUFF

I enjoy giving gifts that people have to wear the minute they open them. Trust me, if you give a birthday girl a tiara, it immediately goes on her head, and then the party can *really* get started! These celebration cuffs are also a hit. It's like a birthday card that you can wear. Now, how fun is that!

## YOU'LL NEED

- 1 piece of fabric (4 inches by 9 inches)
- 1 piece of clear heavy vinyl (4 inches by 9 inches)
- Scissors
- Sewing machine with zigzag stitch
- Printed or handwritten quotes or sentiments (the funnier the better!)
- Curling ribbon
- Confetti
- Paper punches (I used my Fiskars flower punch)
- Fiskars inking shears
- Metal snap set or Velcro dots

*Suggestion:*
Small photos could be fun for this cuff!

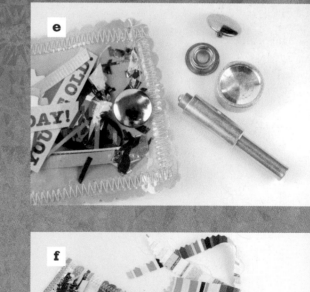

## HeRE's How

**1** Cut the fabric and vinyl into 4-inch by 9-inch pieces. Put the vinyl on top of the fabric and zigzag-stitch around three sides of the rectangle.

**2** Print or write out your quotes or sentiments.

**3** Cut up your curling ribbon, gather your confetti, punch out some colorful flowers, and fill the cuff with all of it through the opening.

**4** Stitch the opening closed.

**5** Cut around the edges with pinking shears.

**6** Add snaps or Velcro dots for the closure.

# COVERED BUTTONS BRACELET

Here's a question: Does a button bracelet have to look like it was made out of buttons? The answer is NO! Introducing the half pearl. I covered up all the holes in my big chunky black buttons and now this button bracelet doesn't look like it's made with buttons. Kind of like magic, wouldn't you say?

## You'll Need

- 20 large flat black buttons
- Drill with $\frac{1}{16}$-inch drill bit
- Piece of scrap wood
- 40 half pearls big enough to cover the holes in the center of the buttons
- E-6000 glue
- 8 inches of chunky gold-tone chain
- Needle-nose pliers (and wirecutters if the pliers don't have them)
- 22 gold-tone jump rings
- 1 gold-tone lobster claw

## Here's How

1. Drill a hole in the outer ridge of all 20 buttons. Make sure to drill on a piece of scrap wood so you don't ruin your counters.

2. Glue a half pearl on both sides of each button with E-6000.

3. Attach the buttons to the chunky gold chain with the jump rings using your needle-nose pliers.

4. Attach jump rings to the ends of the chain and a lobster claw for the closure.

# STEVIE NICKS LEATHER AND LACE

The softness of lace mixed with the toughness of leather. I think it's a perfect combination. Maybe even a little Stevie Nicks. More often than not, I have little pieces of beautiful lace just hanging around my craft room, and I never quite know what to do with them. This was a nice way to use some of the bits and pieces that might have otherwise gone to waste.

## YOU'LL NEED

- Small piece of beautiful lace
- E-6000 glue
- Piece of heavy leather
- Leather hole punch
- 1½ yards of blue leather lace (see Resource Guide)
- Snap set (½-inch)
- X-ACTO knife

### *Hint:*

Use another piece of scrap leather under the leather you are punching so you don't ruin the blade at the end of the leather punch by pushing it into the metal plate below.

340

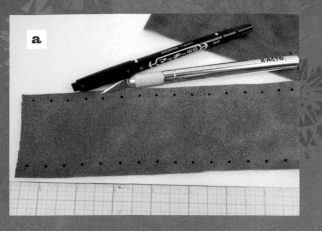

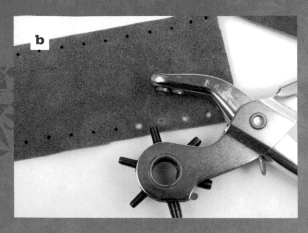

## HERE'S HOW

**1** Cut your leather in a perfect rectangle 3 by 9 inches so that you have a 1-inch overlap on your wrist. I like a wide cuff, but you might like it a bit thinner. Up to you.

**2** Starting ¼ inch from the edge of the leather, mark every ½ inch to the end on both sides as shown in photo a.

**3** Punch holes with the hole punch.

**4** Using a neat layer of E-6000, glue your lace to the center of your leather cuff and let dry. You might want to put a book on top of it to make sure it dries flat. If you do, put some wax paper between the book and the lace just in case some glue seeps out.

**5** Thread your lace through the holes all the way around the cuff.

**6** Glue down the excess on the back of the cuff with a dab of E-6000.

**7** Place snaps on each end of the cuff.

The website www.createforless.com got me hooked on wire and chain. They literally have every kind of craft wire and chain in every different metal tone you could ever want. EVER! I hope my excitement for these two very basic items rubs off on you and that you go nuts like I did. Mix these materials together and watch what happens!

# CRYSTAL CHAIN-LINK NECKLACES

This is perhaps the most conservative piece in this entire book. It's something you could give to your mom or even your grandmother on Mother's Day. In fact, when I'm done writing this, I think I'll send them each one. Trust me on this, it's a lot easier to make than it looks!

## Hint:
You can get stretchy crystal bead bracelets almost anywhere. I got mine at the dollar store and cut them apart. Buy them in tons of different colors and mix them together on the same necklace.

## ★ YOU'LL NEED

- 54 inches of 18-gauge gold wire per necklace
- 25 to 35 crystal beads per necklace
- Needle-nose pliers (and wirecutters if the pliers don't have them)
- Fat marker pen
- 1 gold-tone lobster claw closure

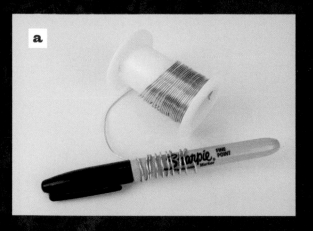

## HERE'S HOW

**1** Cut off 54 inches of gold wire and wrap it around your fat Sharpie marker to make something that looks like a spring.

**2** Slip it off the marker and cut straight through the spring to create large links. (Basically you've created really big jump rings, which you can also use for other projects!)

**3** Slip a crystal bead on a link and close. If the bead doesn't slip entirely on the ring, tuck the other end of the link into the hole in the bead and it will stay.

**4** Continue adding crystal links to form your chain until you've reached your desired length.

**5** Add four to five links without crystals at each end and a lobster claw for the closure.

# BALL AND CHAIN

I couldn't resist calling this one "ball and chain" because, well, it uses ball chain and chain. Plus, if I'm right, it got your attention. Hit the dollar store for plain, flat metal cuffs and go nuts on them with all kinds of bling! All you need is a little E-6000 glue and some imagination.

## YOU'LL NEED

- Plain, flat 2-inch metal cuff
- 22 inches of large-link gold tone chain
- 29 inches of silver-tone ball chain (at any hardware store)
- Needle-nose pliers (and wirecutters if the pliers don't have them)
- E-6000 glue
- Toothpicks
- *Optional:* Transparent tape

## HeRE's HoW

1. Measure the length of your cuff. Across the board, most cuffs I've purchased are about 7 inches from one end to the other.

2. Cut three 7-inch (or the length of your cuff) pieces of the large gold-tone chain.

3. Cut four 7-inch (or the length of your cuff) pieces of the silver-tone ball chain.

4. Starting in the center of the cuff, with dabs of E-6000 on a toothpick, glue gold-tone chains toward one end of the cuff and let dry. If you need them to stick to the sides of the cuff, just tape them down with some transparent tape until it's dry.

5. On the other side, glue the ball chain with E-6000 and let dry.

6. Continue until you've covered the entire cuff.

# LEATHER AND CHAIN

This design is simple and unisex. If you don't want to use chain, you might try twine or even leather lacing. I like the mixture here and think that a man could wear this just as easily as a woman. Hang a charm or two from it and you have an entirely different project.

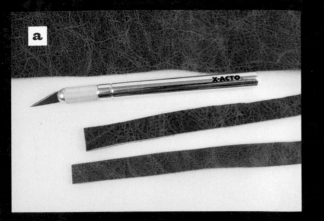

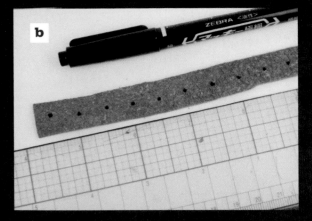

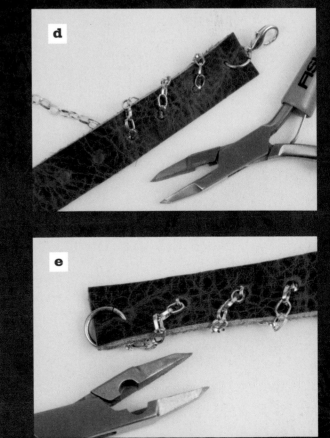

## YOU'LL NEED

- Strip of leather (at least 16 inches long and ¾ inch wide)
- Leather hole punch
- Piece of scrap leather
- 1 yard of fine silver- or gold-tone chain
- 2 jump rings to match your chain
- 1 large lobster claw closure per choker or bracelet

## HERE'S HOW

**1** Measure around your neck and cut a leather strip ¾ inch wide and the length you want. Make sure it's comfortable.

**2** On the back of the leather, starting ¼ inch from the edge, mark every ½ inch all along the center of the leather.

**3** Punch holes where you marked all along the strip of leather with a leather punch. Put a scrap piece of leather underneath your strip to keep your punch sharp and prevent it from hitting the metal every time you punch a hole.

**4** Cut 2 yards of chain if it's not already cut and connect the end of your chain to the end hole with a jump ring, then thread the chain through each hole around the edge to the other end.

**5** Attach jump rings to the ends of the chains and a lobster claw for the closure.

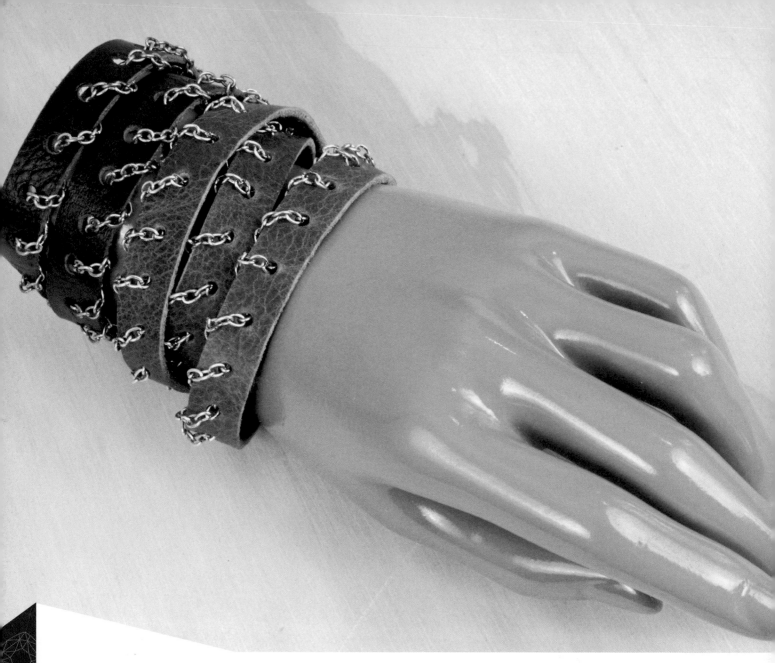

## FOR THE BRACELETS

**1** Repeat steps 1 through 5, but use a shorter
length for your wrist, or a longer piece
if you'd like it to wrap around your wrist
several times.

# BEAD ON A WIRE

Hit the dollar store or the hardware store for different wires that you can use in your jewelry making and go crazy with it. Once you get the hang of this project, you'll be using all kinds of different combinations.

*Hint:*
You can get stretchy crystal bead bracelets almost anywhere. I got mine at the dollar store and cut them apart. Buy them in tons of different colors and mix them together on the same necklace.

## YOU'LL NEED

- 2 yards of 18-gauge galvanized or silver-tone wire per necklace
- 25 to 35 crystal beads per necklace
- Needle-nose pliers (and wirecutters if the pliers don't have them)

## HERE'S HOW

1. Cut the wire into about 26 pieces that are anywhere from 2 to 2½ inches long.
2. With your needle-nose pliers, make a loop on one end of a piece of wire big enough for another wire to slip through.
3. Slip a crystal bead on the wire and make a loop.
4. Slip the other end of the wire through the first loop and bend another loop around it so that it locks together.
5. Keep adding crystal beaded links to form your chain until you've reached your desired length.
6. Make sure you make it long enough to slip over your head.

# CRYSTAL TASSEL EARRINGS

These are supereasy to make and bursting with style. Change the color of the crystal or the tone of chain, and you'll have something to match every outfit in your wardrobe.

# YOU'LL NEED

- 2 yards of fine silver-tone chain
- Needle-nose pliers (and wirecutters if the pliers don't have them)
- 2 silver-tone jump rings
- 2 crystal beads
- 4 inches of 20-gauge wire
- 2 silver-tone earring wires

# HERE'S HOW

**1** Cut the chain in twenty-four 3-inch pieces.

**2** Thread twelve chain pieces on a jump ring.

**3** Cut two 2-inch pieces of the wire and bead a crystal on each wire. Bend a loop on one end and another loop on the other end to attach to the earring wire.

**4** Place the jump ring with the 12 chains on the bottom loop of crystal.

**5** Repeat for the other earring.

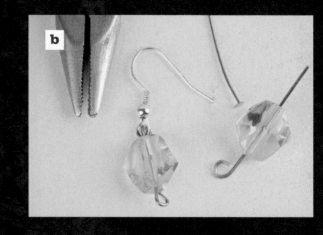

# WATERFALL CHAIN CHOKER

I feel like this is something that Carrie from *Sex and the City* would wear. It's dramatic and definitely makes a statement. You could almost wear it as a necktie with a button-down shirt . . .

Be sure to visit www.createforless.com for amazing chains of every kind.

## YOU'LL NEED

- 14 yards of fine gold-tone chain
- 14 inches of medium gold-tone chain
- 5 links of large gold-tone chain
- Needle-nose pliers (and wirecutters if the pliers don't have them)
- 9 gold-tone jump rings
- 1 gold-tone lobster claw closure

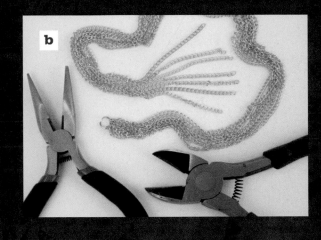

## HERE'S HOW

**1** Cut seven 14-inch pieces of thin gold chain and loop them onto a jump ring.

**2** Repeat step 1 four times.

**3** Cut two 7-inch pieces of medium chain and connect one on each side of the large five-link piece of chain.

**4** Add jump rings and a lobster claw for the back.

**5** Add each set of seven 14-inch chains to the five large links in the center of your choker.

*Hint:*
Try mixing different metal tones together to give a seriously funky feel to this project.

# THINGS I USED

These are great items to have around the house for whenever you get inspired. Don't forget to consult the Resource Guide, too, for suggestions on where to find some of these things and many more of the less common items.

**ALUMINUM FLASHING:** This comes in a roll in different widths. It's great for the tin projects because it's easy to cut (see *Tin shears*) and holds its shape when it's bent. Also, it doesn't rust!

**BEADING WIRE:** Want your beaded projects to be around forever? Use beading wire. It's a thin wire coated in plastic and it's stronger than Atlas!

**BOBBY PINS:** Pick them up at any 99-cent store in tons of different colors or just stick to plain old black and spray paint them!

**BOOKS, OLD AND DISCARDED:** You can use the paper for all sorts of things. Cut up pages for decoupage projects, mount artwork on a book page background, or use the covers for card-stock—there are tons of possibilities. They're always very handy as weights while you're drying glue work on handbags, jackets, and so on.

**BUCKETS WITH LIDS:** Great for storing large batches of papier-mâché and for keeping water and sponges nearby while you work.

**BUTTONS:** Start collecting these now and try always to have tons around. Get them anywhere and glue them on anything. They are decorative, great for flower centers, and neat for mosaic projects.

**CLEAR PLASTIC TUBING:** Sold at hardware stores for plumbing. This can be cut into different sizes to create beads for some terrific accessories. I wrapped some in chain and loved the results.

**CLOTHESPINS, WOOD, AND PLASTIC:** Wooden clothespins are perfect for gluing around and on projects to give them a handmade feel, and the plastic ones are great little clamps for holding things together while they dry.

**CRAFT KNIVES:** X-ACTO works for me! I use tons of these. Use them for making clean cuts, scoring, and preserving as much detail as you can while cutting out images.

**CUTTING MAT:** This is a piece of plastic that you can use your craft knife on, over and over again, without harming it. It's perfect for all of the precise cutting you do. It also has a 1-inch-square grid for easy measuring. Once again, Fiskars makes the best.

**DECORATIVE SCISSORS:** You can get these in so many different shapes. Fiskars has an amazing selection and you will want them all. They give your paper projects beautiful borders. (Also see *Pinking shears*, and *Fiskars* in the Resource Guide.)

**DRILL AND DRILL BITS:** Get a good drill. Mine is from Skil, and it's sturdy and strong. A nice selection of drill bits will last you forever, as long as you take care of them (Black & Decker make a great set). Stay away from cheap tools; they just don't last!

**ELMER'S GLUE-ALL:** The basic white stuff is great for all craft projects, especially decoupage.

**ELMER'S WOOD GLUE:** For small wood projects, when getting a small nail in place is sometimes impossible, this stuff will really keep your work together. It's also great for securing pieces of furniture that might be wobbly. Just fill in the cracks, and you'll see what a difference it makes! I use it all the time on old furniture.

**EMBOSSING POWDERS AND EMBOSSING PAD:** Traditionally used with rubber stamps to give a raised image. This powder is activated with heat and comes in an endless array of colors. You can get it at any craft store. Press your rubber stamp in the pad and press it on your paper, then sprinkle on your powder. Remove the excess and heat the image covered in powder to get the effect. It's fantastic!

**EXTENSION CORDS:** Let's just say that sometimes your glue gun does not quite reach your worktable.

**FABRIC:** I save all scraps and eventually use every last one.

**FAUX FLOWERS AND LEAVES:** Stick them in vases, use them for jewelry, spruce up a headband . . . always have tons around, they will come in handy.

**FELT AND STICKY FELT:** Just a great fabric that does not fray at the edges. Use it for adhering to the bottoms of your projects so they don't scratch the surfaces of your tables, for graphic fabric projects such as pillows and tablecloths, for appliqués so you don't have to use pins while you are sewing, and a million other uses.

**GLITTER GLUE:** Createforless.com has a great selection of this sparkly stuff. Glitter glue is perfect for sprucing up any project. I love it and never leave the house without some in my backpack!

**GLUE STICKS:** What did we do without them? Perfect for greeting card and envelope projects. A nice clean way to use glue.

**GOOGLE.COM (IMAGE SEARCH FEATURE):** If you're looking for a picture of a Union Jack to make a pillow pattern or need an image of Frida Kahlo to transfer onto a pillow, these days you can just get on your computer and do an image search. What an easy way to find inspiration for your projects!

**E-6000 GLUE:** Eclectic products has a huge selection of different glues that bond everything. The E-6000 is the best—it sticks just about anything to anything.

**GUTTER GUARD:** This plastic material with a grid pattern can be used for all kinds of projects. It's fun to experiment with. I guess whatever you have left over could actually be used for your gutter, too!

**HAMMER:** A must for every toolbox. Try a smaller craft hammer for tiny nails and projects.

**HOT GLUE GUN AND GLUE STICKS:** You can get these anywhere. Although I am not a huge fan of the hot glue gun, there are great things you can do with it, and as long as you use another adhesive along with it, it's perfect for keeping something in place.

**JIGSAW WITH SEVERAL BLADES**: I use a Skil jigsaw with a scroll blade or fine blade for many of my projects.

**MAGAZINES:** Old magazines are full of inspiring pictures and great ideas for new projects.

**MARBLES:** Glass chips and mosaic tiles. All terrific for jewelry making and wonderful for the glass-fusing projects.

**METALLIC SPRAY PAINTS, GOLD AND SILVER:** As any Southern girl will tell you, everything looks better sprayed silver and/or gold. Krylon's metallic spray paints are my favorite.

**NEEDLE-NOSE PLIERS:** Super for picking up tiny things and bending small wires. There are very delicate ones for jewelry, but also sturdier ones that still let you do fine tasks and also have wirecutters, and these are really useful.

**NEWSPAPERS:** You need these to keep your work area clean, for papier-mâché and paper turquoise, and for inspiration.

**PAINTBRUSHES:** Get them anywhere, in lots of sizes, and make sure you take care of them.

**PAINT THINNER:** This stuff is flammable, so be careful. It's great for getting rid of all kinds of messes, and can even remove some gooey glue. Just dab a bit on a cotton swab, and you have a very useful item.

**PAPER CLIPS:** In case you need a wire hook, these are handy to have around. Just unbend them and twist them into shape. They're also great materials to use in your crafts—I always have gold, silver, and multicolor ones around.

**PAPERCUTTER:** Perfect for making straight edges and long cuts. It's also great for cutting several sheets at once. Get one at Staples for a good price.

**PAPER SHREDDER:** I got one on sale at Staples for fifteen dollars. Great for making huge batches of paper strips for your papier-mâché projects, paper turquoise, etc.

**PAPER TOWELS AND OLD RAGS:** The more messes I create, the more I need a lot of cleanup supplies on hand, and I'll bet you will, too.

**PARCHMENT PAPER:** Great for work surfaces if you want to keep them clean, and wonderful for fusing plastic bags together.

**PENCILS:** You can never have enough pencils. You'll use them for marking measurements, tracing, sketching, outlining . . .

**PINKING SHEARS:** Shears with notched blades; used to finish edges of cloth with a zigzag cut for decoration or to prevent raveling or fraying. I love them! I have one pair for paper and one pair for fabric, and both are made by Fiskars. (Also see *Decorative Scissors,* and *Fiskars* in the Resource Guide.)

**PINS:** Flathead pins or ball-point pins will help keep your things in place while they dry.

**PLYWOOD, BIRCH, ¼-INCH, ½-INCH, ¾-INCH, AND 1-INCH THICKNESS:** Great for all of your wood projects. Birch plywood has a nice finish and is a higher grade than other plywood.

**POPSICLE STICKS AND WOODEN COFFEE STIRRERS:** Use these for mixing paints, stirring resin, you name it.

**Q-TIPS:** Perfect for dabbing on small bits of glue or taking off a little drip of paint while you work.

**RECYCLED CONTAINERS:** C'mon, how many times have you needed something to store your brushes and pencils in? Use what you have around the house.

**RIBBON:** Great for finishing edges on projects, hanging picture frames the old-fashioned way, and embellishing pretty much anything. Keep lots of different kinds on hand—satin (shiny), grosgrain (ribbed), faille (sheer), wired, novelty—and stock a variety of widths.

**ROCKS TO USE AS PAPERWEIGHTS:** It's always good to have some smooth rocks on hand to hold things down while you work. I work outside a lot, and I just gather some and keep them beautifully arranged in a corner somewhere. You'll be surprised at how handy they are.

**RULERS:** Have a few on hand at all times. You will need them for everything. Be sure to get a metal ruler for making cuts with your craft knives.

**SAFETY GOGGLES OR GLASSES:** It doesn't matter if you are only drilling or sawing or hammering for one second. You need to protect your eyes!

**SAFETY PINS:** What would we do without them? Not only are they useful, but used for jewelry and embellishing, they are just wonderful! Grab as many as you can when you see them!

**SANDPAPER:** I like to sand items before applying glue or paint to them. The rough surface it gives will give the glue something to stick to, and a little sandpaper is perfect for scoring.

**SCISSORS FOR PAPER AND FABRIC:** Invest in your fabric scissors (Fiskars makes the best scissors). For paper, it's good to have several pairs, so you don't have to waste your time sharpening. (Also see *Decorative scissors* and *Pinking shears*, and *Fiskars* in the Resource Guide.)

**SCREWDRIVER SET:** No home should be without a set of screwdrivers. Paint the tops of the Phillips-head screwdrivers one color so that you know what you are picking up from the tool can. I swear, whenever I want a Phillips I grab a flathead, and vice versa!

**SCREWS AND NAILS:** Small, long, fat, wood, metal, these will always be useful.

**SCRUBBERS:** You know how messy you can be. Always have some small ones on hand.

**SEWING MACHINE:** Need I say more?

**SHARPIE PERMANENT MARKERS:** These will write on most any surface, so try to have them around. I like to use them on metal.

**SPRAY ADHESIVE:** Elmer's makes a wonderful spray adhesive. It's a spray glue that gives a nice, even coat of glue on your projects. There are strong- and light-tack ones, and depending on the tack, you can reposition your work until it dries, which is very helpful when you're decoupaging images.

**SPRAY BOTTLE:** Next time you empty out a spray bottle of glass cleaner, save it and fill it with water for your workroom. Spraying water on your projects that use paint can produce wonderful effects. It can cloud ink and make spray paint gather and dry into terrific patterns.

**STAPLER:** You'd be surprised how you can use your stapler for projects in ways other than stapling a pile of papers together.

**TAPE:** Painter's tape, masking tape, transparent tape. You need them all! Have plenty around for your projects.

**THRIFT STORES:** A great place to find old jewelry pieces to take apart. Look for things like belts and mismatched earrings that have small pieces you can use for your creations.

**TIN SHEARS:** Hand shears for cutting sheet metal. There are so many beautiful projects in this book that use sheets of aluminum. You will want to have a nice pair of shears that cuts with a serrated edge so the edges are not sharp.

**TOOTHPICKS:** Great for getting glue in just the right spot. Perfect for jewelry-making!

**TURPENTINE:** Great for cleaning oil-base paint off brushes.

**TWINE:** From tying up your recycled newspapers into bundles to creating a very cool fringe edge. Twine is your friend, and now it comes in fantastic colors. Mason Twine, for example, is a nylon twine that comes in neon colors. Stock up and use it!

**WAX PAPER:** I don't craft without it! It's the perfect work surface, since glues and resins don't stick to it. Keep it around if you tend to be a little messy with the glue bottle.

**WIRECUTTERS:** Get a pair with spring action. They are much easier to work with. This way, you have more control when you are working on your projects.

**WIRE, SMALL-, MEDIUM-, AND HEAVY-GAUGE:** I'm constantly wiring things together and twisting wires into sculptures and other structures. Keep some around for everyday use and in case you get inspired. (www.createforless.com has an amazing selection.)

**WOOD SCRAPS:** Check out the scrap pile of a local wood worker to see if you can get a bag of scrap wood for a good price.

**WORK GLOVES IN COTTON, CANVAS, LEATHER, AND RUBBER:** Find a pair that fits, so that you can really use your fingers.

**3-D CRYSTAL LACQUER OR MOD PODGE DIMENSIONAL MAGIC:** This is an alternative to coating something with resin. It's nontoxic and has a nice finish. To find it, check online or at your local craft store. Also, www.amazon.com carries it.

# RESOURCE GUIDE

**THE CONTAINER STORE ◆ www.containerstore.com**

I rely on this place to keep myself organized and when I want to find containers for all my creations.

**WWW.CREATEFORLESS.COM**

This is ALWAYS my first stop for anything I need to create my craft projects. The prices are amazing and the selection is incredible!

**DIAMOND TECH ◆ www.diamondtechcrafts.com**

The makers of Fuseworks Microwave Kiln Kit. I'm in love with this product! This is an amazing way to make beautiful fused glass pieces.

**ECLECTIC PRODUCTS ◆ www.eclecticproducts.com**

The makers of E-6000. I can't get through a craft project without this glue. It's simply the best for all of your crafting needs. Get a tube or two immediately!

**FISKARS ◆ www.fiskars.com**

The best scissors, hands down! For every cutting need you have, Fiskars has a product for you. Their shaped paper punches are pretty amazing, too! www.createforless.com carries them in case you're not able to find them in your area.

**DOLLAR (AND 99-CENT) STORES**

What a great resource for just about anything you might need. Glass plates, candles, toothpicks, Popsicle sticks—you name it. You can't depend on the stock, but more often than not, you will find a piece of your crafting puzzle there for only a buck (or 99 cents).

**ELMER'S GLUE PRODUCTS ◆ www.elmers.com**

You can find Elmer's almost anywhere, but just in case you want to see what else the company makes and sells in bulk, this is a good place to start. I like to buy the white glue (Elmer's Glue-All) by the gallon, since I use so much of it.

**GLU-STIX.COM**

This is the most comprehensive hot glue gun site on the web. Calling their toll-free Customer Service line (1-877-770-5500) connects you directly to one of their "Glue Professionals," who are there every day to help customers find the right glue or gun for every purpose.

**GOODWILL AND SALVATION ARMY STORES**
**www.goodwill.org ◆ www.salvationarmy.org**

If you need a table or handbag or jacket or shoes and you're prepared to add a little pizzazz to them, or looking for a chair to spruce up and paint, this is the place to go. The money goes to a good cause, and it's fun to recycle something. Check out these places before you head off to a furniture or clothing store for something brand new.

**GROCERY STORE**

I know this is obvious, but I like to be thorough.

**THE HOME DEPOT ◆ www.homedepot.com**

You can get anything here, from lamp-making parts to lumber. It's a great place to roam around and get inspired.

**LUMIERE PAINTS ◆ www.jacquardproducts.com**

The Lumiere paints are my favorites. They are water-base acrylics, metallic, have tons of pigment (and come in gorgeous colors), and apply beautifully.

### JOANN FABRICS ◆ www.joann.com

Terrific national fabric chain with wonderful remnants at great prices. They carry every sewing notion and most paper and craft supplies you could ever need!

### KRYLON ◆ www.krylon.com

Krylon products are available everywhere. They truly are the best paints and spray paints around. They dry easily and make a great finish. Krylon has everything you can imagine—plus a few things you probably never imagined—from frosted-glass paint to reflective paint to make-your-own-mirrors. Their Glitter Blast paint has been a crafting sensation and their metallic paints are absolutely top-notch!

### LOWE'S ◆ www.lowes.com

It's a joy to shop at Lowe's. It's organized, the staff is knowledgeable, and you can find just about anything you need there for your projects, plus ideas for more.

### MINWAX ◆ www.minwax.com

You know I love these products. They are quality products for all your woodworking needs. I can't get through a craft project without the Poly-crylic clear coat as a finish. Even when it's not made of wood. *Shhhh!* I discovered something amazing recently. If you spray-paint something and it remains tacky, spray it with the Minwax Clear Aerosol Lacquer and the problem is gone as soon as it dries.

### ORIENTAL TRADING COMPANY ◆ www.orientaltrading.com

More than twenty-five thousand fun products for every occasion! Great online resource for craft supplies. If you can't find something, try this site.

### PEARL RIVER ◆ www.pearlriver.com

The perfect place for all your Asian craft materials, from lanterns to fabrics. If you are going for an Asian theme, start by checking out this site. They ship everywhere, and the prices are great!

### SKIL ◆ www.skil.com

These are the only power tools I use for my projects. They are of a good quality, fairly priced, and powerful. The sanders are my favorite because you can handle them easily, and the drills are fantastic. I promise you will be happy with any Skil tool you purchase.

### SWAROVSKI CRYSTALS ◆ www.swarovski.com

If you want to kick your projects up a notch and use the world's BEST crystals, check out Swarovski! Every project in this book will look even more amazing if you add a little Swarovski. Trust me on this! They can be pricey, but for a piece of jewelry you want to wear for years to come, I think it's worth the investment.

### TRASH BIN

I believe that we have to recycle as much as we can, so why not start by using what we discard to make our projects? Cans and tins, boxes, yogurt cups, plastic soda bottles—they are all perfect starts to many projects.

### WWW.VINTAGEJEWELRYSUPPLIES.COM

Beautiful antique brass, copper and silver stampings. Butterflies, birds, bees, crowns—you name it, they have something that will fit your taste.

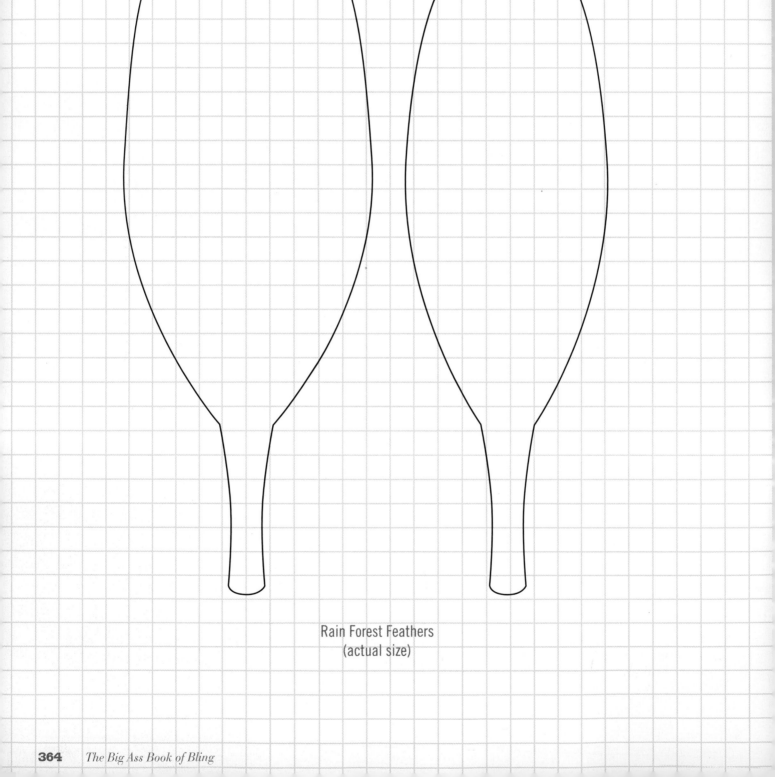

Rain Forest Feathers
(actual size)

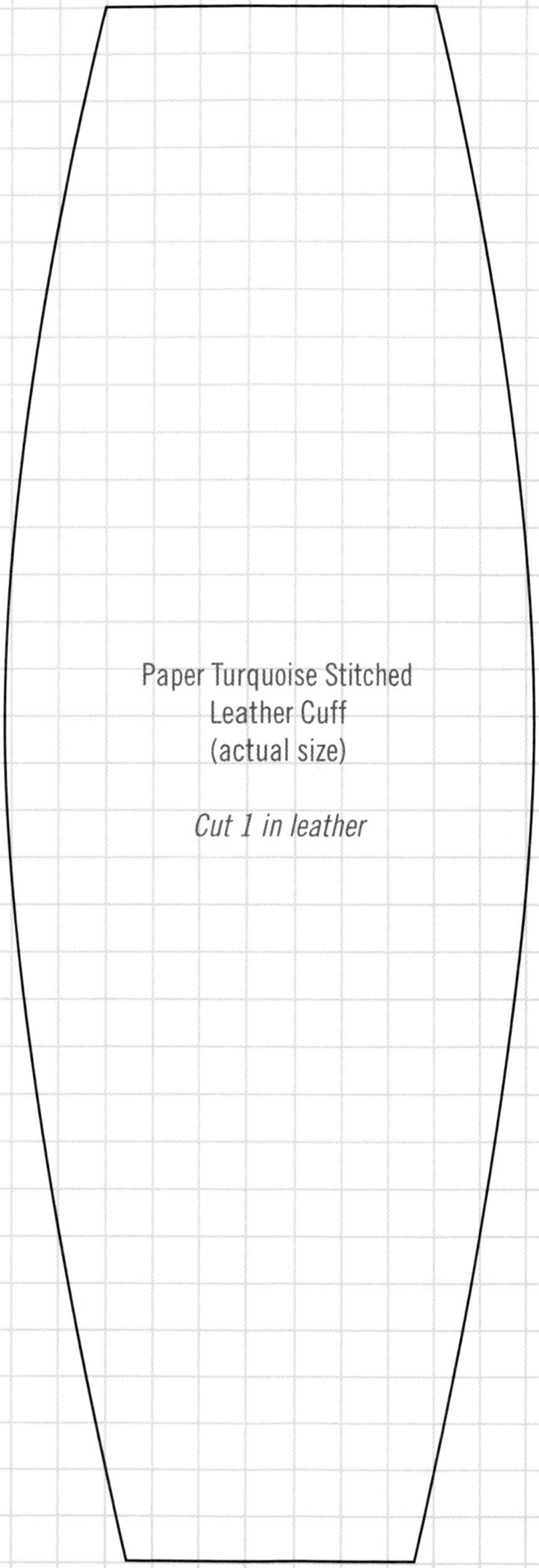

Paper Turquoise Stitched
Leather Cuff
(actual size)

*Cut 1 in leather*

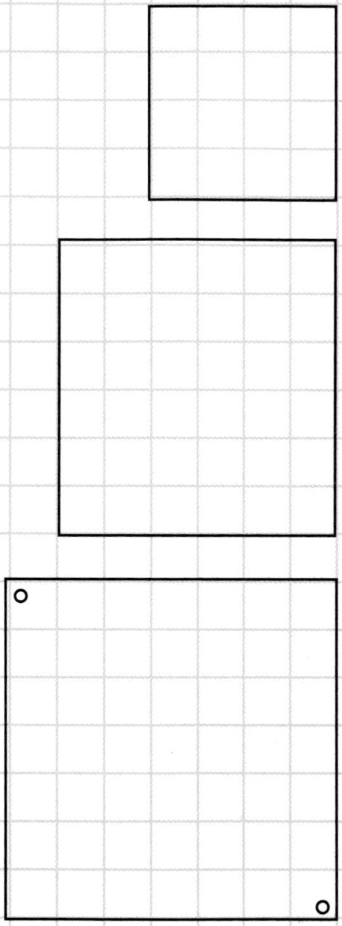

Squares on Turquoise Conch
(actual size)

*Cut in cardboard*

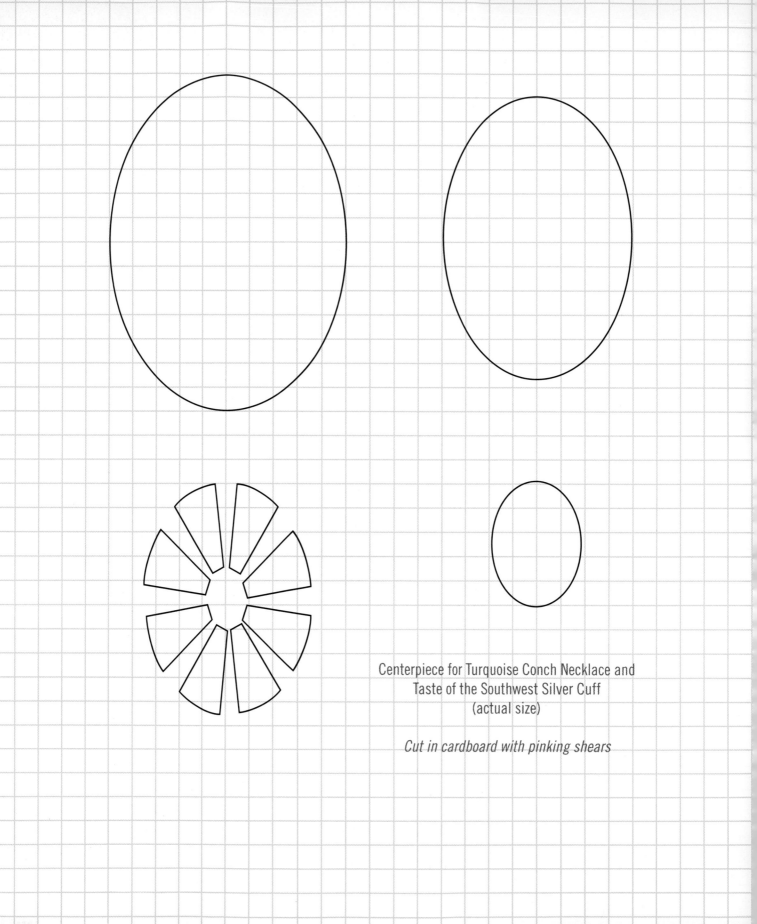

Centerpiece for Turquoise Conch Necklace and
Taste of the Southwest Silver Cuff
(actual size)

*Cut in cardboard with pinking shears*

Scrappy Flower Hat Pin
(actual size)

Vinyl Flower Patterns
(actual size)

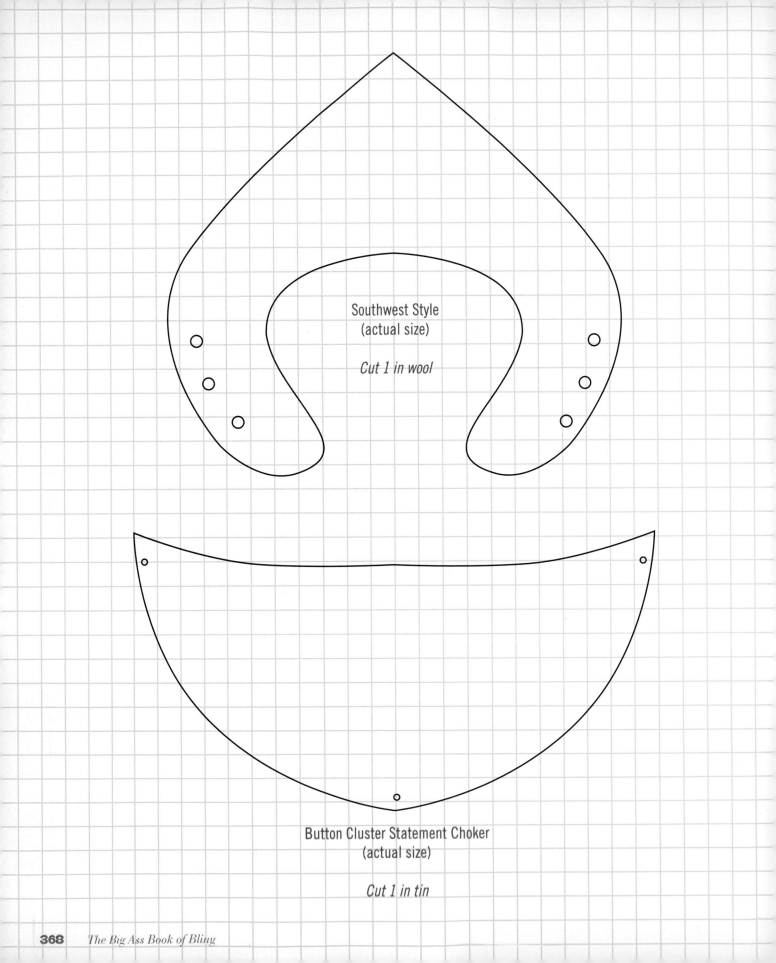

Southwest Style
(actual size)

*Cut 1 in wool*

Button Cluster Statement Choker
(actual size)

*Cut 1 in tin*

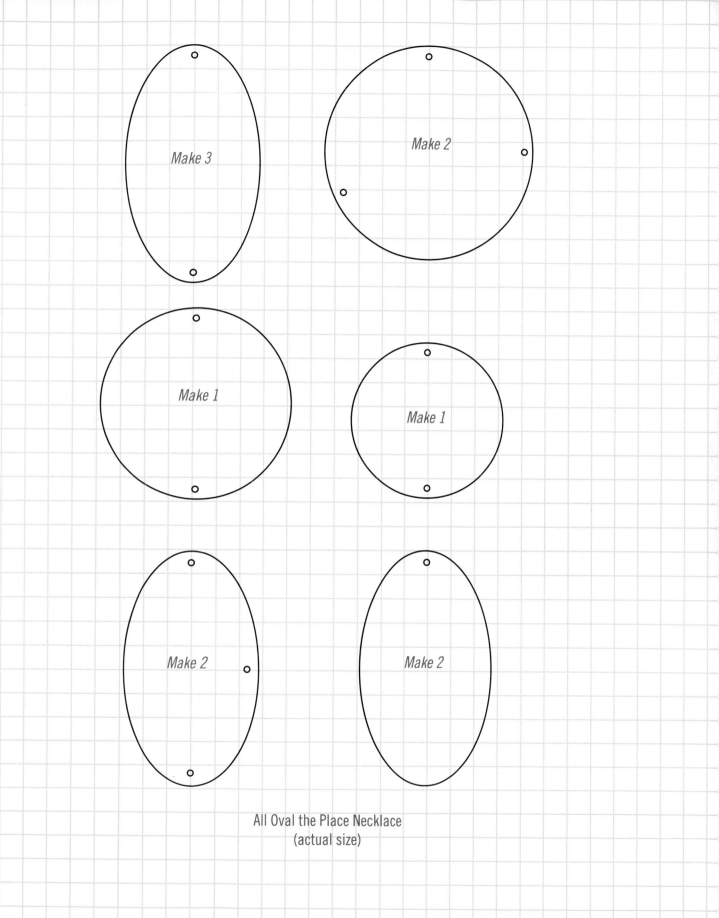

Make 3

Make 2

Make 1

Make 1

Make 2

Make 2

All Oval the Place Necklace
(actual size)

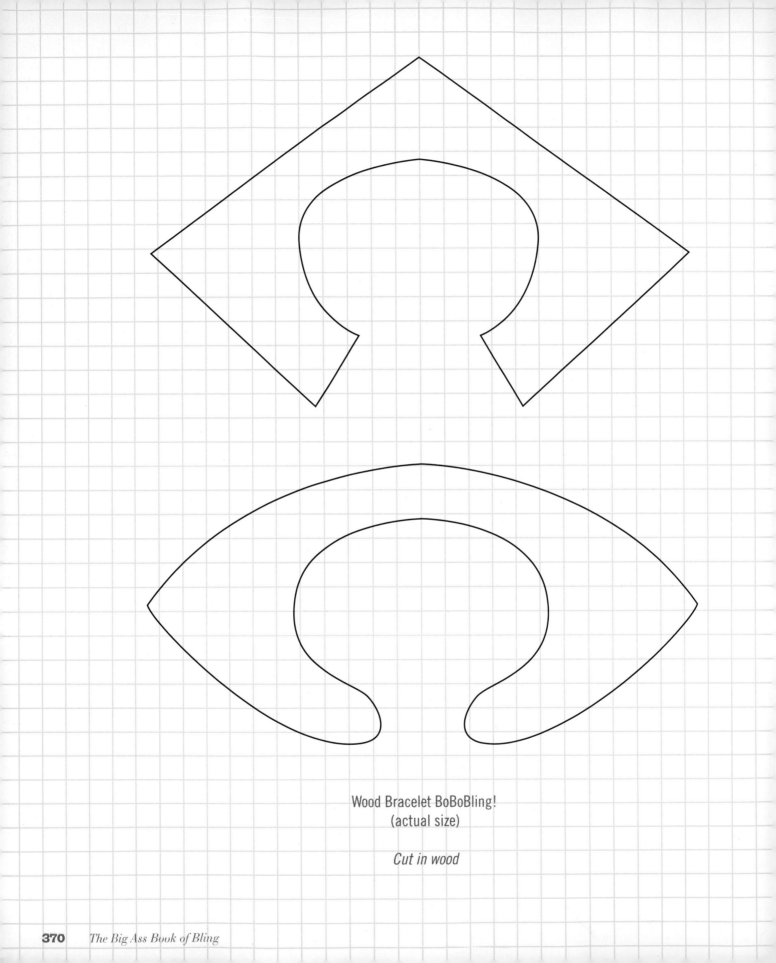

Wood Bracelet BoBoBling!
(actual size)

*Cut in wood*

Wood Bracelet for BoBoBling!
(actual size)

*Cut in wood*

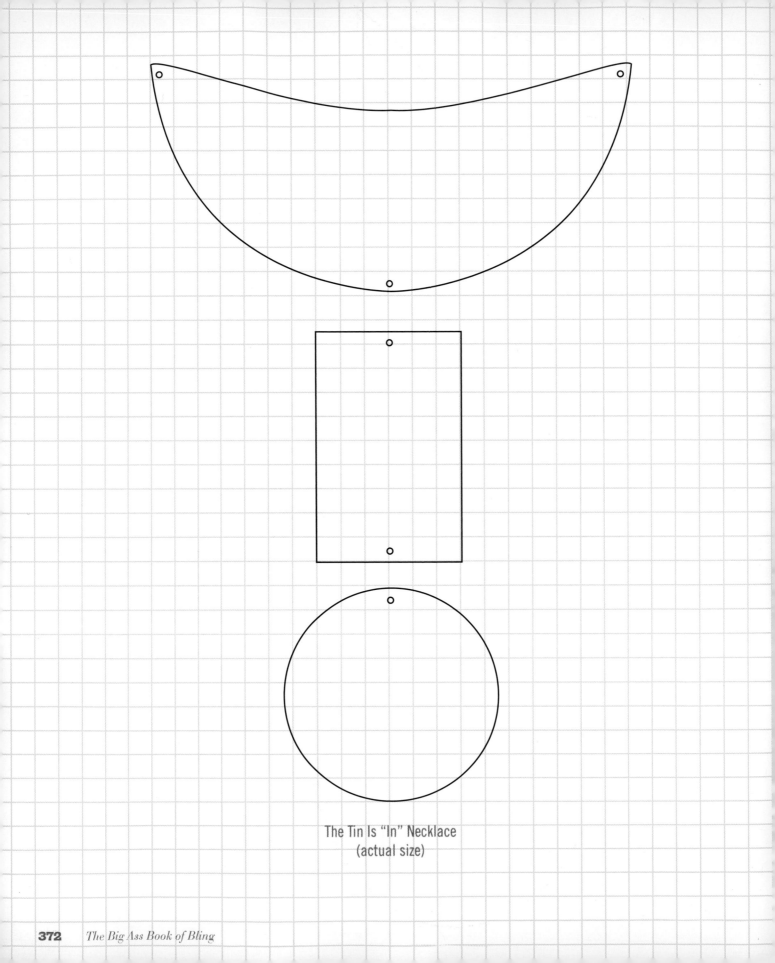

The Tin Is "In" Necklace
(actual size)

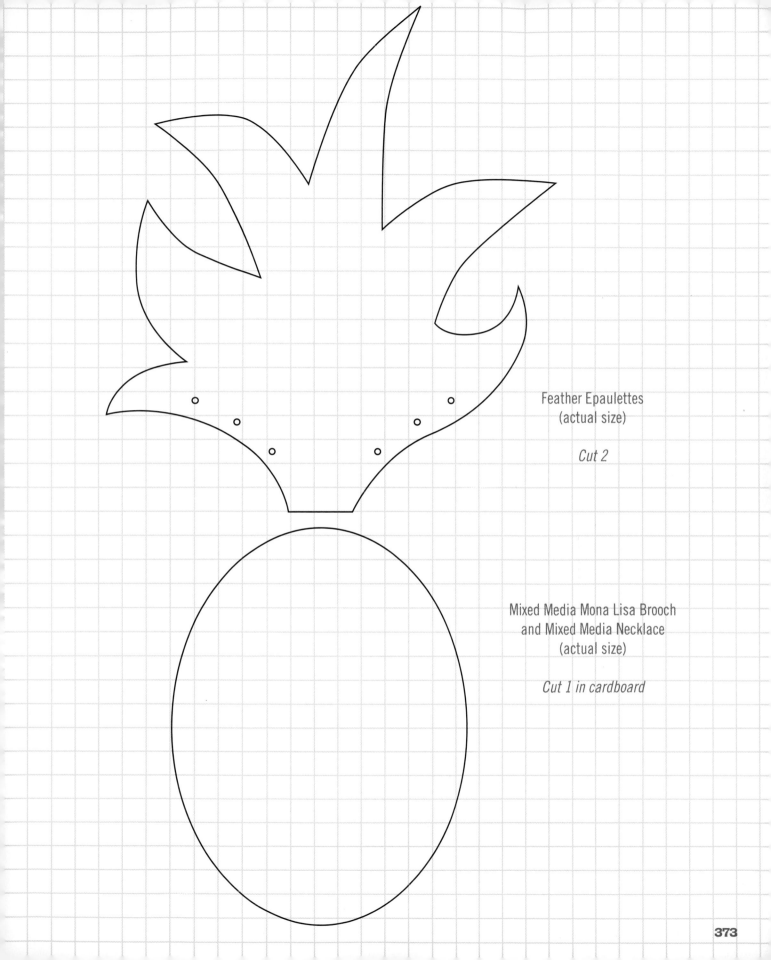

Feather Epaulettes
(actual size)

*Cut 2*

Mixed Media Mona Lisa Brooch
and Mixed Media Necklace
(actual size)

*Cut 1 in cardboard*

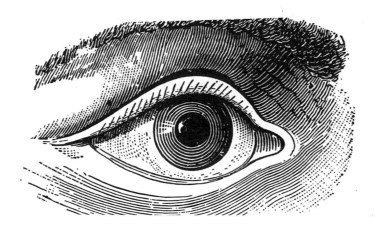

# GOT A CRAFTY QUESTION?
# STILL ITCHING FOR INSPIRATION?
# VISIT MARK ON THE WEB AT:

MARKMONTANO.COM
MARKMONTANOBLOGS.BLOGSPOT.COM
TWITTER.COM/MARKMONTANO
FACEBOOK.COM/MARKMONTANONYC
YOUTUBE.COM/USER/MAKEYOURMARKMONTANO

And don't forget to check out *The Big-Ass Book of Crafts*!

And *The Big-Ass Book of Crafts 2*!

OVER 150 CRAFTS TO FILL YOUR HOME, GIVE TO FRIENDS, DECORATE THE YARD, OR SEND TO MOM.

THE BIG-ASS BOOK of CRAFTS

BY MARK MONTANO   PHOTOGRAPHS BY 

MORE THAN 150 PROJECTS TO DECORATE YOUR DIGS, SPOIL YOUR FRIENDS, LIVEN YOUR LANDSCAPE, OR SEND TO MOM!

THE BIG-ASS BOOK of CRAFTS 2

BY MARK MONTANO   BIGGER, BETTER, SASSIER!

GALLERY BOOKS
A Division of Simon & Schuster
A CBS COMPANY

www.simonandschuster.com